# BATMAN
## THE BAT AND THE BEAST

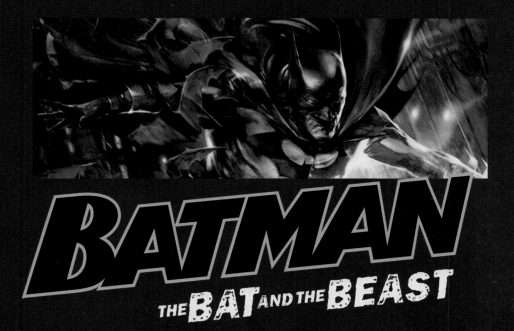

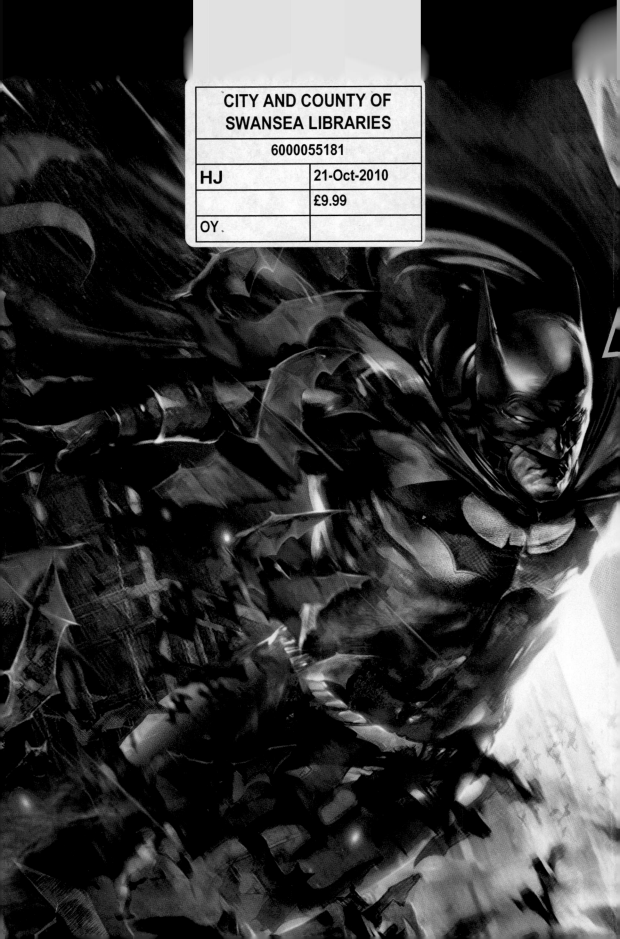

# BATMAN

## THE BAT AND THE BEAST

**Peter Milligan**
Writer

**Andy Clarke**
Artist

**David Baron**
Colorist

**Sal Cipriano**
Letterer

**Jock**
Cover Artist

Batman created by Bob Kane

**Mike Marts** Editor-original series
**Janelle Siegel** Assistant Editor-original series
**Bob Harras** Group Editor-Collected Editions
**Peter Hamboussi** Editor
**Robbin Brosterman** Design Director-Books

DC COMICS
**Diane Nelson** President
**Dan DiDio** and **Jim Lee** Co-Publishers
**Geoff Johns** Chief Creative Officer
**Patrick Caldon** EVP-Finance and Administration
**John Rood** EVP-Sales, Marketing and Business Development
**Amy Genkins** SVP-Business and Legal Affairs
**Steve Rotterdam** SVP-Sales and Marketing
**John Cunningham** VP-Marketing
**Terri Cunningham** VP-Managing Editor
**Alison Gill** VP-Manufacturing
**David Hyde** VP-Publicity
**Sue Pohja** VP-Book Trade Sales
**Alysse Soll** VP-Advertising and Custom Publishing
**Bob Wayne** VP-Sales
**Mark Chiarello** Art Director

BATMAN: THE BAT AND THE BEAST
Published by DC Comics. 

DC Comics, 1700 Broadway, New York, NY 10019
A Warner Bros. Entertainment Company
Printed by World Color Press, Inc., Dubuque, USA. 7/28/10. First printing.
ISBN: 978-1-4012-2794-4

Cover by Guillem March

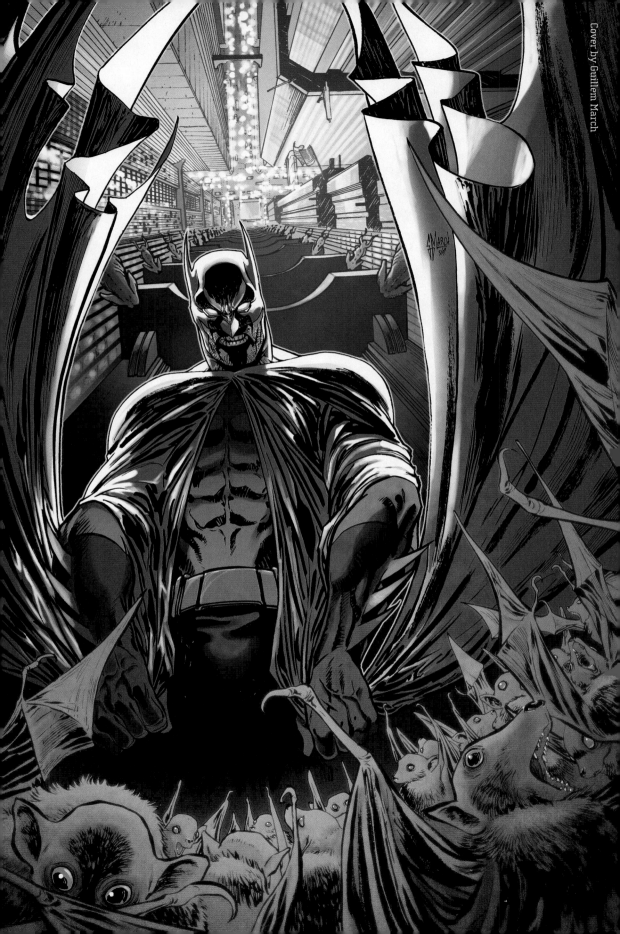

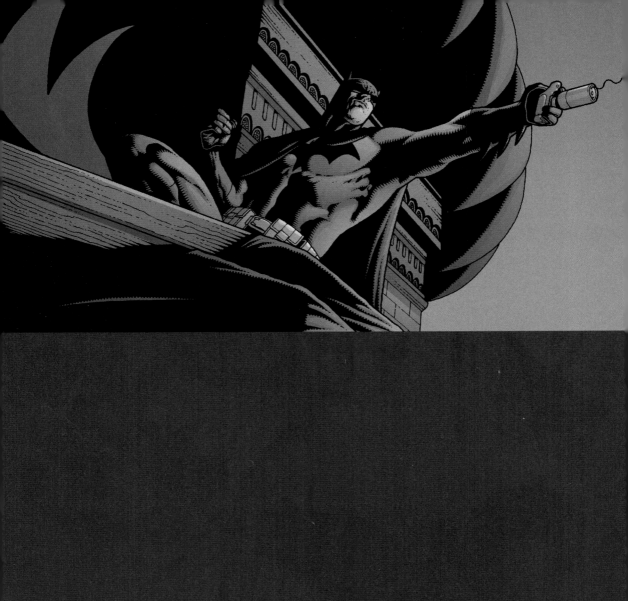

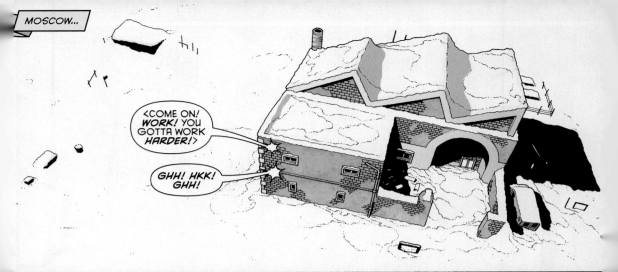

<COME ON! *WORK!* YOU GOTTA WORK *HARDER!*>

GHH! HKK! GHH!

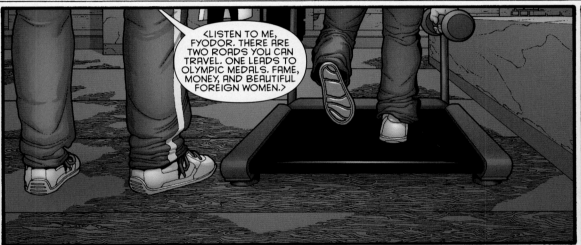

<LISTEN TO ME, FYODOR. THERE ARE TWO ROADS YOU CAN TRAVEL. ONE LEADS TO OLYMPIC MEDALS. FAME, MONEY, AND BEAUTIFUL FOREIGN WOMEN.>

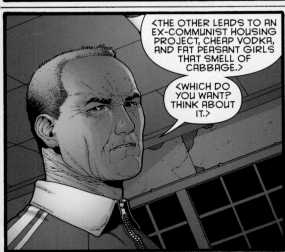

<THE OTHER LEADS TO AN EX-COMMUNIST HOUSING PROJECT, CHEAP VODKA, AND FAT PEASANT GIRLS THAT SMELL OF CABBAGE.>

<WHICH DO YOU WANT? THINK ABOUT IT.>

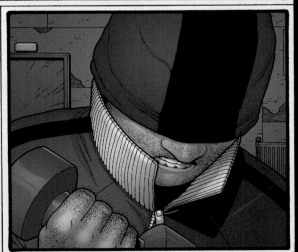

# THE BAT AND THE BEAST

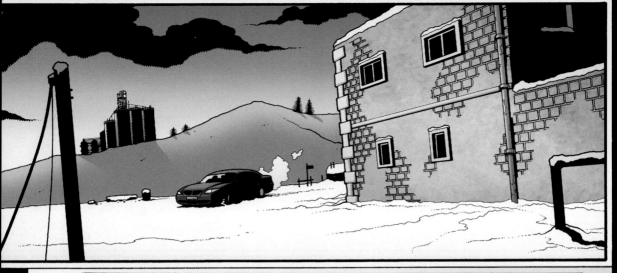

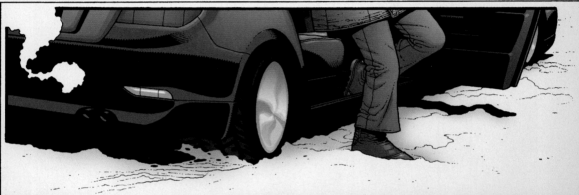

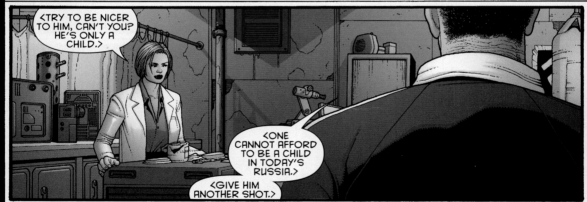

<TRY TO BE NICER TO HIM, CAN'T YOU? HE'S ONLY A CHILD.>

<ONE CANNOT AFFORD TO BE A CHILD IN TODAY'S RUSSIA.>

<GIVE HIM ANOTHER SHOT.>

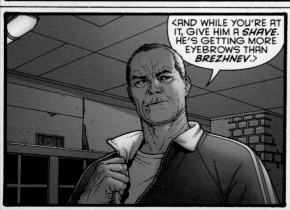

<AND WHILE YOU'RE AT IT, GIVE HIM A *SHAVE*. HE'S GETTING MORE EYEBROWS THAN *BREZHNEV*.>

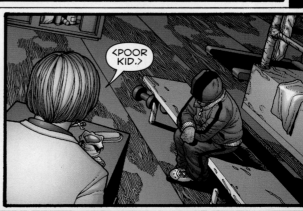

<POOR KID.>

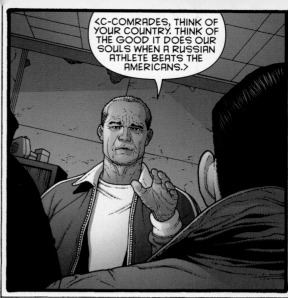

<C-COMRADES, THINK OF YOUR COUNTRY. THINK OF THE GOOD IT DOES OUR SOULS WHEN A RUSSIAN ATHLETE BEATS THE AMERICANS.>

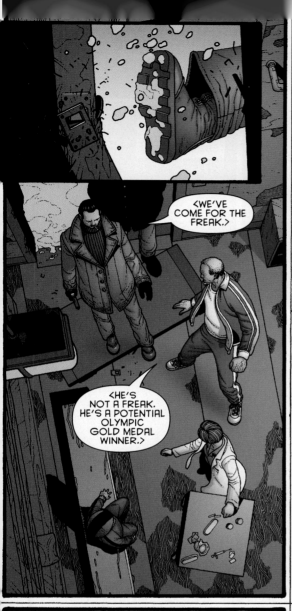

<WE'VE COME FOR THE FREAK.>

<HE'S NOT A FREAK. HE'S A POTENTIAL OLYMPIC GOLD MEDAL WINNER.>

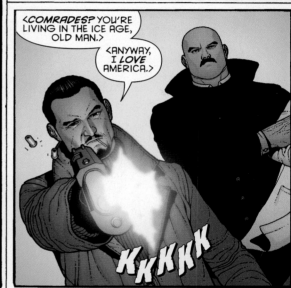

<COMRADES? YOU'RE LIVING IN THE ICE AGE, OLD MAN.>

<ANYWAY, I LOVE AMERICA.>

KKKKK

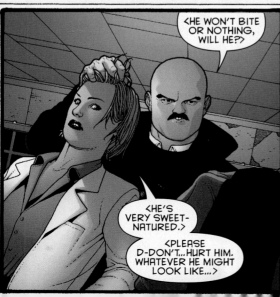

<HE WON'T BITE OR NOTHING, WILL HE?>

<HE'S VERY SWEET-NATURED.>

<PLEASE D-DON'T...HURT HIM. WHATEVER HE MIGHT LOOK LIKE...>

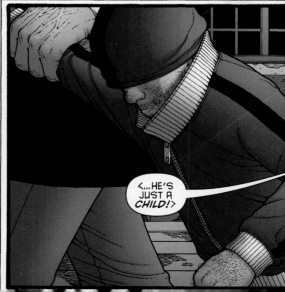

<...HE'S JUST A CHILD!>

TWELVE YEARS LATER...
<"BEAUTIFUL!">
<"EXQUISITELY, UNBEARABLY BEAUTIFUL.">
<MADE BY PETER CARL FABERGÉ IN 1901 FOR TSAR NICHOLAS II. AND NOW THE LATEST TSAR GIVES IT TO YOU.>
<HAPPY SEVENTEENTH BIRTHDAY, FYDOR!>
<EXTRAVAGANT, YES... BUT I KNOW HOW YOU LOVE FABERGÉ.>
<AND YOU'VE BEEN SO GOOD LATELY WITH MY LITTLE PROBLEMS.>

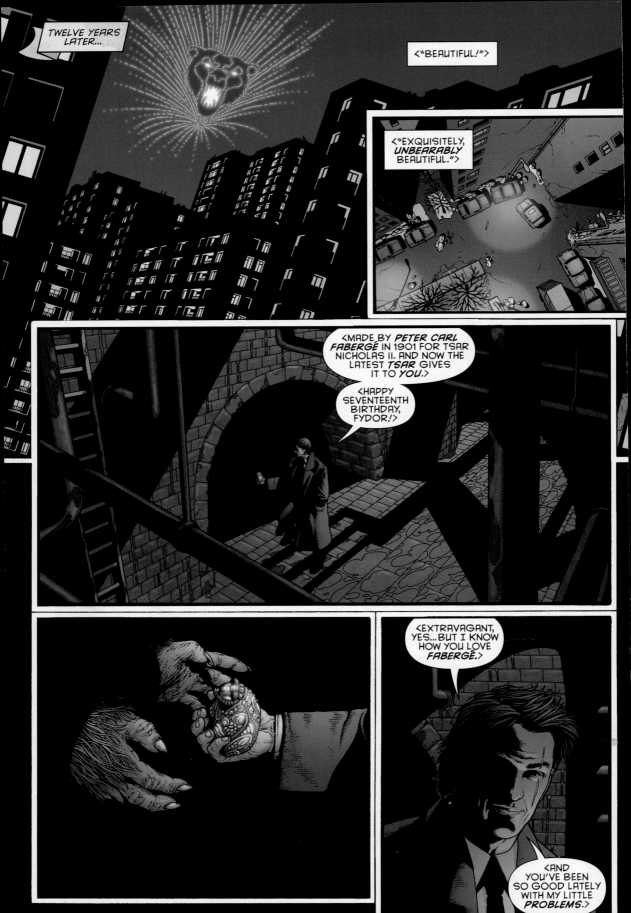

<MAY I BE BRUTALLY HONEST WITH YOU?>
<IT'S JUST THAT...EVERY TIME I COME DOWN HERE THE STINK GETS WORSE. AND THOSE RAT DROPPINGS...THEY REALLY ARE ***REVOLTING***.>
<YOU DON'T HAVE TO LIVE LIKE THIS, BOY.>
<I COULD FIND YOU A NICE QUIET APARTMENT IN A SMART PART OF THE CITY.>
<WHAT IS IT YOU'RE TRYING TO ***PROVE***, HM?>
<BUT MAYBE APARTMENT-LIVING ISN'T YOUR STYLE, EH? MAYBE...MAYBE LIVING IN THIS SQUALOR MAKES THE FABERGÉS I GIVE YOU SEEM EVEN MORE BEAUTIFUL.>
<LIFE IS ALL IN THE ***CONTRAST***, IS IT NOT?>
<LOOK, I DON'T WANT TO SPOIL YOUR BIRTHDAY WITH BUSINESS, BUT...>
<...YOU KNOW WHAT I WAS SAYING... ABOUT YOU HELPING ME WITH MY LITTLE PROBLEMS...?>

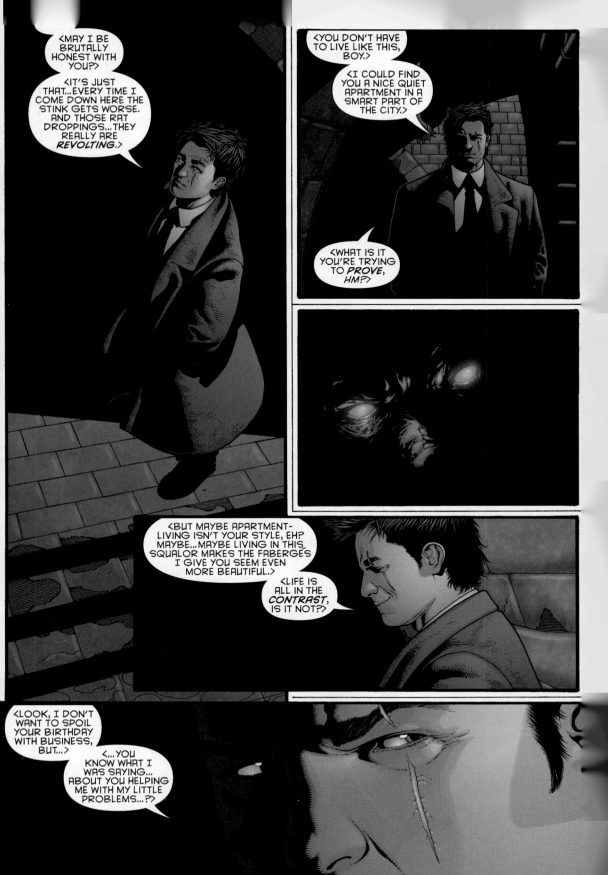

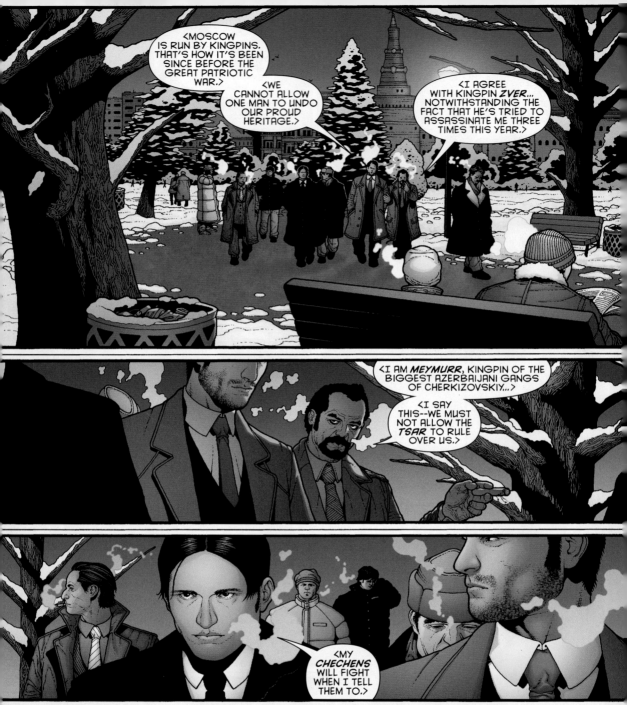

<MOSCOW IS RUN BY KINGPINS. THAT'S HOW IT'S BEEN SINCE BEFORE THE GREAT PATRIOTIC WAR.>

<WE CANNOT ALLOW ONE MAN TO UNDO OUR PROUD HERITAGE.>

<I AGREE WITH KINGPIN ZVER... NOTWITHSTANDING THE FACT THAT HE'S TRIED TO ASSASSINATE ME THREE TIMES THIS YEAR.>

<I AM MEYMURR, KINGPIN OF THE BIGGEST AZERBAIJANI GANGS OF CHERKIZOVSKIY...>

<I SAY THIS--WE MUST NOT ALLOW THE TSAR TO RULE OVER US.>

<MY CHECHENS WILL FIGHT WHEN I TELL THEM TO.>

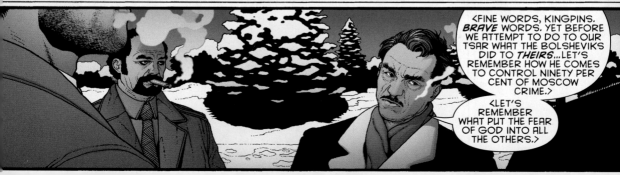

<FINE WORDS, KINGPINS. BRAVE WORDS. YET BEFORE WE ATTEMPT TO DO TO OUR TSAR WHAT THE BOLSHEVIKS DID TO THEIRS...LET'S REMEMBER HOW HE COMES TO CONTROL NINETY PER CENT OF MOSCOW CRIME.>

<LET'S REMEMBER WHAT PUT THE FEAR OF GOD INTO ALL THE OTHERS.>

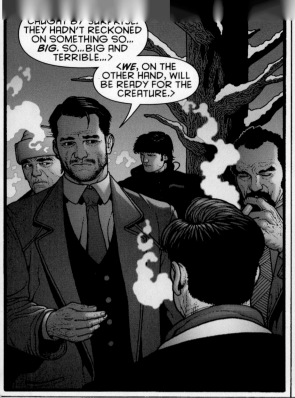

CAUGHT BY SURPRISE. THEY HADN'T RECKONED ON SOMETHING SO... *BIG*. SO...BIG AND TERRIBLE...⟩

⟨*WE*, ON THE OTHER HAND, WILL BE READY FOR THE CREATURE.⟩

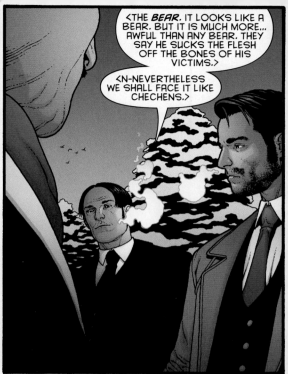

⟨THE *BEAR*. IT LOOKS LIKE A BEAR. BUT IT IS MUCH MORE... AWFUL THAN ANY BEAR. THEY SAY HE SUCKS THE FLESH OFF THE BONES OF HIS VICTIMS.⟩

⟨N-NEVERTHELESS WE SHALL FACE IT LIKE CHECHENS.⟩

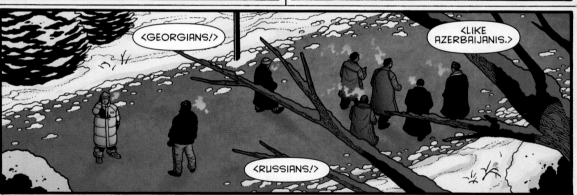

⟨GEORGIANS!⟩

⟨RUSSIANS!⟩

⟨LIKE AZERBAIJANIS.⟩

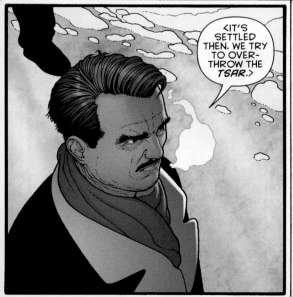

⟨IT'S SETTLED THEN. WE TRY TO OVER-THROW THE *TSAR*.⟩

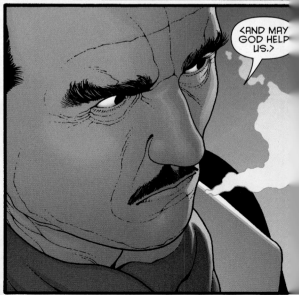

⟨AND MAY GOD HELP US.⟩

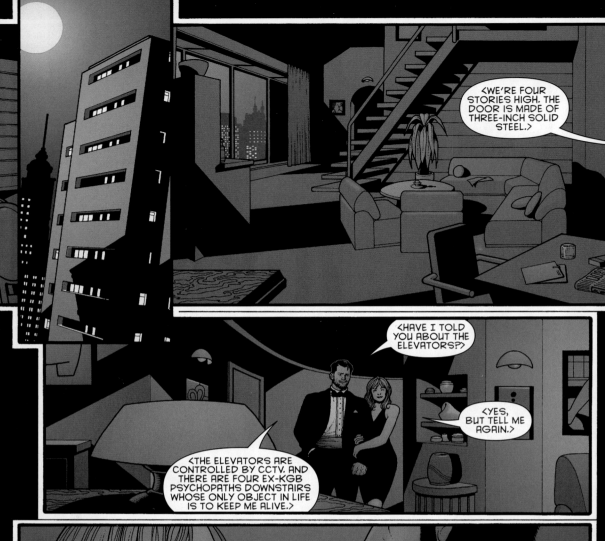

<WE'RE FOUR STORIES HIGH. THE DOOR IS MADE OF THREE-INCH SOLID STEEL.>

<HAVE I TOLD YOU ABOUT THE ELEVATORS?>

<YES, BUT TELL ME AGAIN.>

<THE ELEVATORS ARE CONTROLLED BY CCTV. AND THERE ARE FOUR EX-KGB PSYCHOPATHS DOWNSTAIRS WHOSE ONLY OBJECT IN LIFE IS TO KEEP ME ALIVE.>

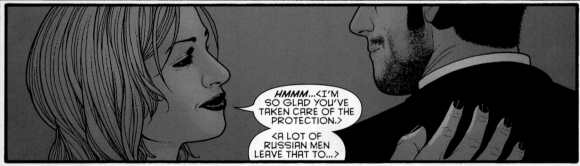

HMMM...<I'M SO GLAD YOU'VE TAKEN CARE OF THE PROTECTION.>

<A LOT OF RUSSIAN MEN LEAVE THAT TO....>

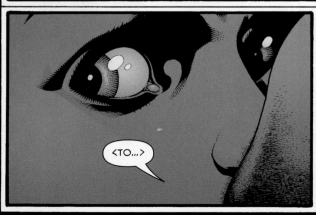

<TO....>

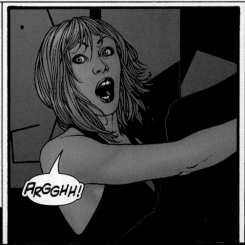

ARGGHH!

<OH MY GOD.>
<H-HOW? HOW DID YOU... GET PAST MY BOYS?>
BLAMM BLAMM BLAMM
GNNG! <NO! PLEASE. NO!>
UGHN UGH UGH UGGN...

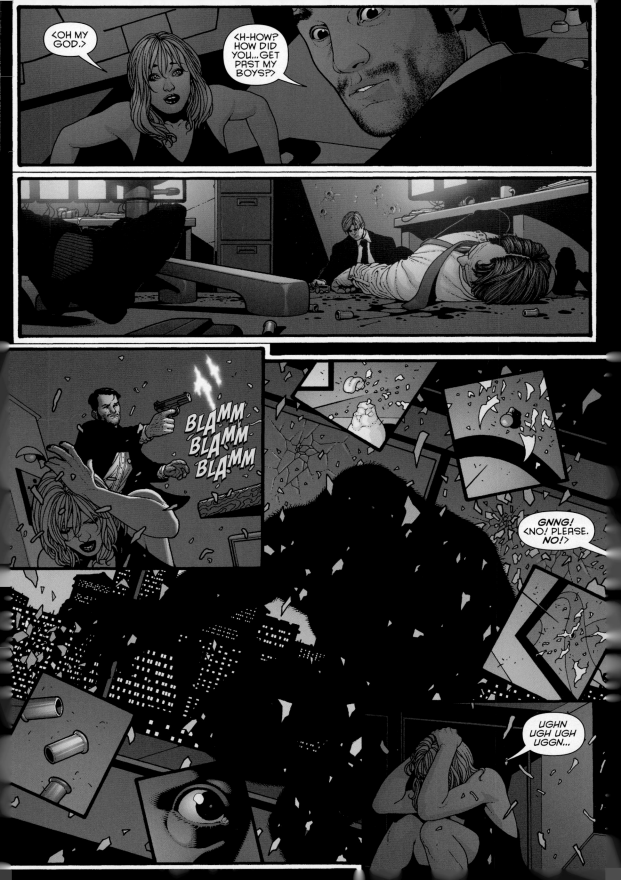

ARGHHH!
AH... AHGG... AGHHH...

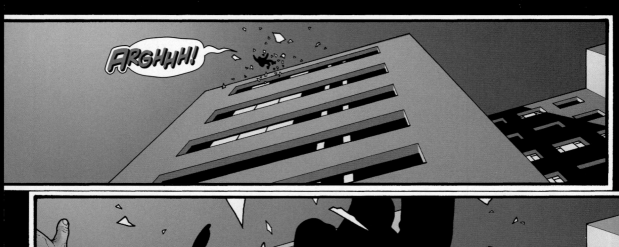

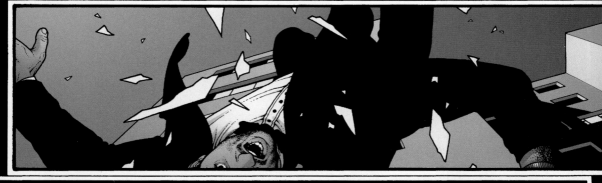

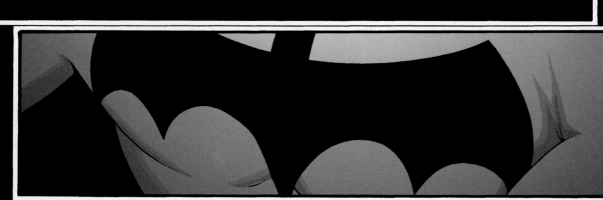

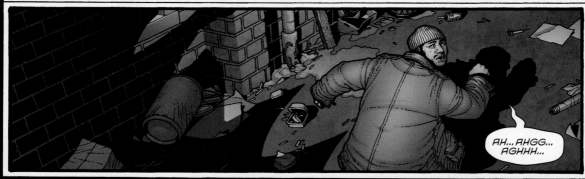

YOU'RE OUT OF SHAPE, MORRINO.
UGNN!
IS... HGHH... THAT WHAT YOU CHASE ME... TWO...
HUHH... TWO BLOCKS TO TELL ME?
I KNOW I'M OUTTA SHAPE.
I GOT HIGH BLOOD PRESSURE, DEGENERATIVE BONE DISEASE, AND MY CHOLESTEROL'S OFF THE SCALE. BUT Y'KNOW WHAT?
I'M HAPPY.
TELL ME ABOUT THE RUSSIAN.
UH-UH. NO CAN DO. SWORN TO SILENCE. OMERTO. IF I SAY ONE WORD...
THE RUSSIAN, MORRINO.
OR I CHASE YOU UP AND DOWN EVERY STREET IN GOTHAM.

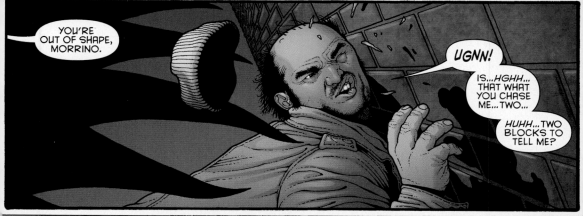

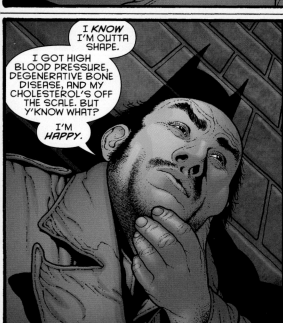

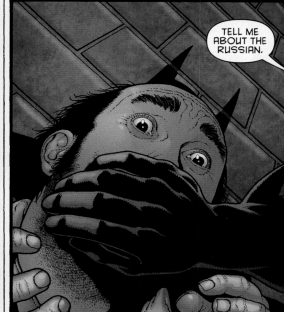

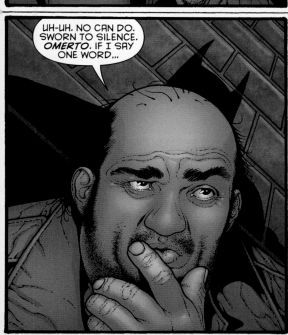

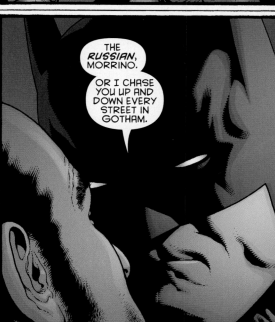

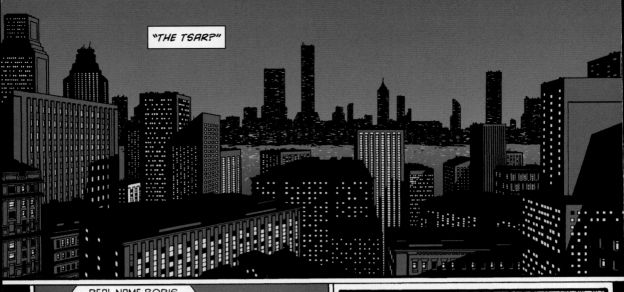

"THE TSAR?"

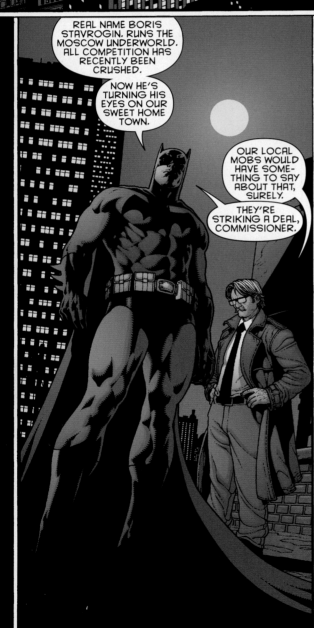

REAL NAME BORIS STAVROGIN. RUNS THE MOSCOW UNDERWORLD. ALL COMPETITION HAS RECENTLY BEEN CRUSHED.

NOW HE'S TURNING HIS EYES ON OUR SWEET HOME TOWN.

OUR LOCAL MOBS WOULD HAVE SOMETHING TO SAY ABOUT THAT, SURELY.

THEY'RE STRIKING A DEAL, COMMISSIONER.

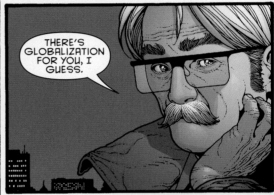

THERE'S GLOBALIZATION FOR YOU, I GUESS.

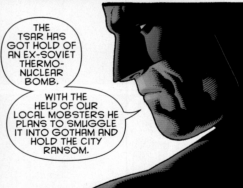

THE TSAR HAS GOT HOLD OF AN EX-SOVIET THERMO-NUCLEAR BOMB.

WITH THE HELP OF OUR LOCAL MOBSTERS HE PLANS TO SMUGGLE IT INTO GOTHAM AND HOLD THE CITY RANSOM.

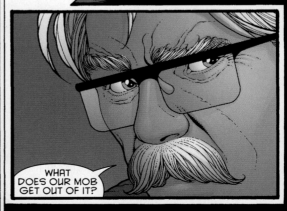

WHAT DOES OUR MOB GET OUT OF IT?

THE TSAR SPLITS THE RANSOM WITH THEM. OUR MOB GUESSES HE'LL TRY TO TAKE OVER THE GOTHAM UNDERWORLD. BUT THEY THINK THEY CAN CONTROL HIM.
NEED ANY HELP WITH THIS?
Denison's
I JUST THOUGHT YOU SHOULD KNOW ABOUT IT.
RIGHT. GOOD LUCK, THEN.
NOT THAT YOU EVER NEED IT.
THE TSAR.
OH, BOY.

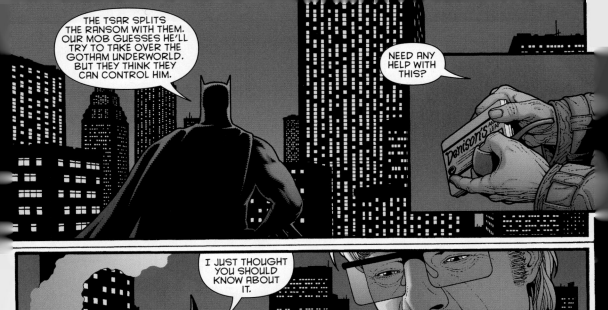

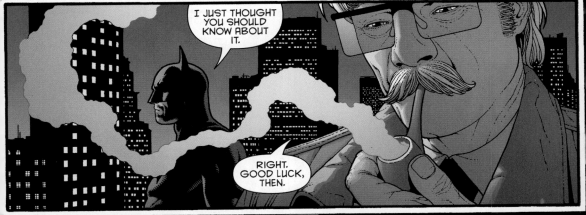

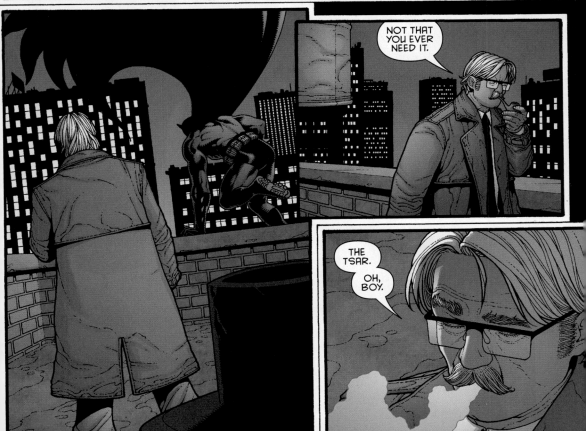

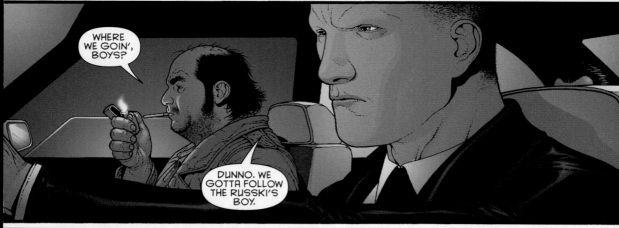

WHERE WE GOIN', BOYS?

DUNNO. WE GOTTA FOLLOW THE RUSSKI'S BOY.

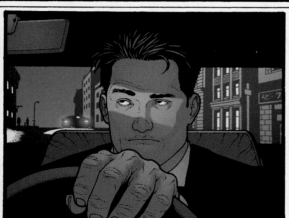

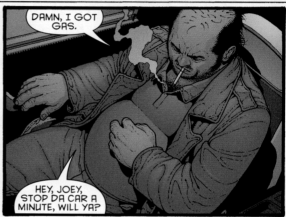

DAMN, I GOT GAS.

HEY, JOEY, STOP DA CAR A MINUTE, WILL YA?

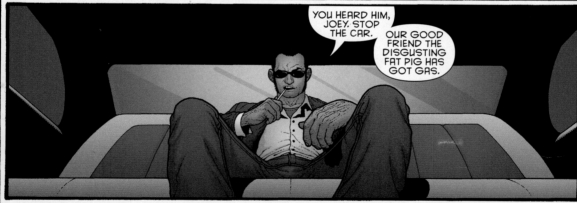

YOU HEARD HIM, JOEY. STOP THE CAR.

OUR GOOD FRIEND THE DISGUSTING FAT PIG HAS GOT GAS.

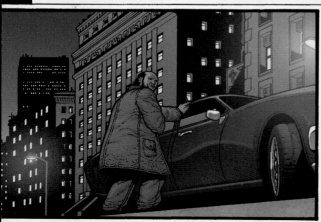

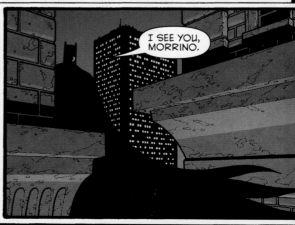

I SEE YOU, MORRINO.

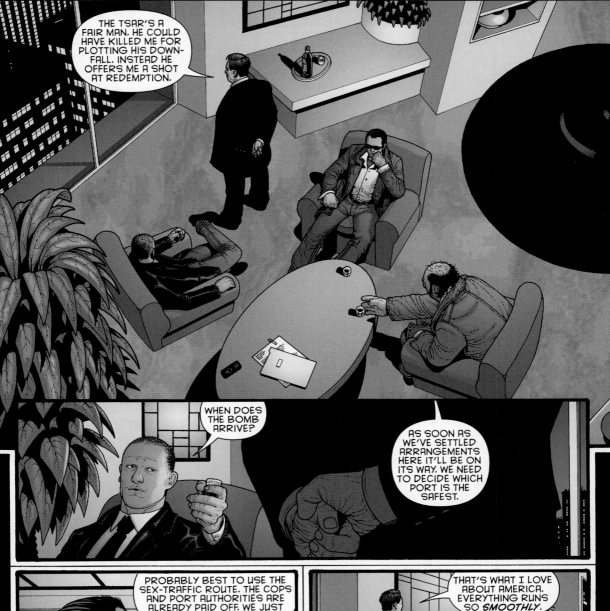

THE TSAR'S A FAIR MAN. HE COULD HAVE KILLED ME FOR PLOTTING HIS DOWNFALL. INSTEAD HE OFFERS ME A SHOT AT REDEMPTION.

WHEN DOES THE BOMB ARRIVE?

AS SOON AS WE'VE SETTLED ARRANGEMENTS HERE IT'LL BE ON ITS WAY. WE NEED TO DECIDE WHICH PORT IS THE SAFEST.

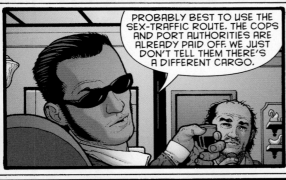

PROBABLY BEST TO USE THE SEX-TRAFFIC ROUTE. THE COPS AND PORT AUTHORITIES ARE ALREADY PAID OFF. WE JUST DON'T TELL THEM THERE'S A DIFFERENT CARGO.

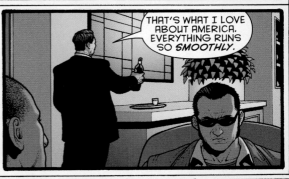

THAT'S WHAT I LOVE ABOUT AMERICA. EVERYTHING RUNS SO SMOOTHLY.

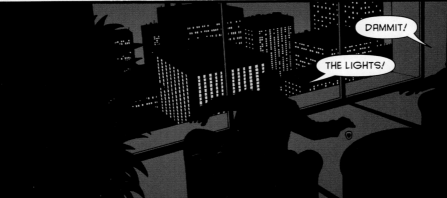

DAMMIT!

THE LIGHTS!

GET THOSE DAMNED LIGHTS ON!
MYSKIN, IF THIS IS SOME KINDA TRICK...
TOLDYA WE SHOULDN'T TRUST NO RUSSIAN.


PUT YOUR GUN DOWN, SANTO. IT'S A BLACK OUT, THAT'S--
OH, HOLY--

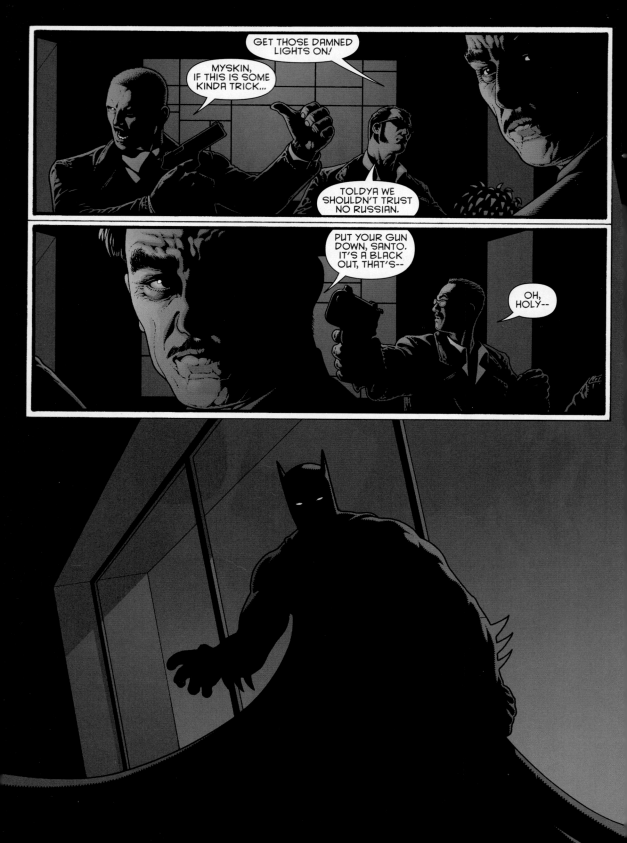

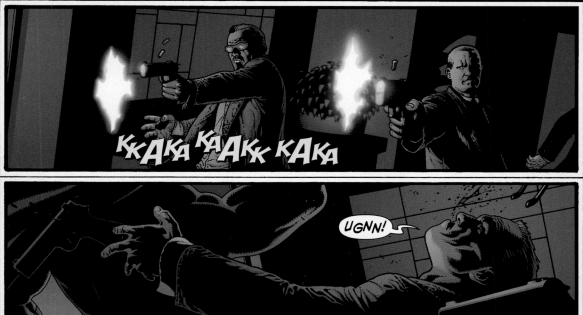

KKAKA KAAKK KAKA

UGNN!

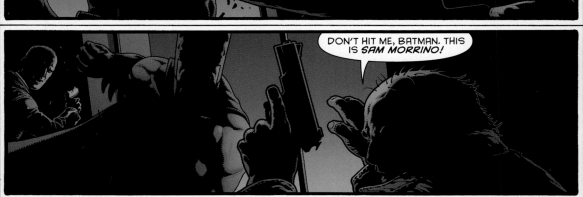

DON'T HIT ME, BATMAN. THIS IS *SAM MORRINO!*

FAT MAN, YOU LOUSY SNITCH!

I'M A GOTHAMITE, JOEY--WHY SHOULD I HELP SOME *RUSSIAN* BLOW UP MY CITY?

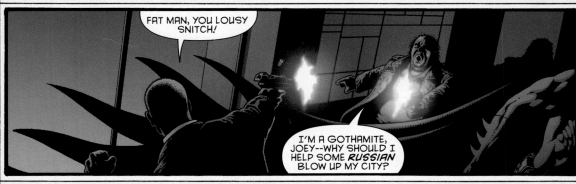

UGHH HGHH HGG

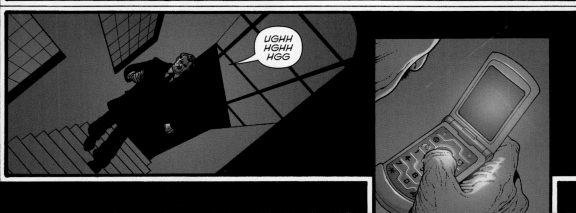

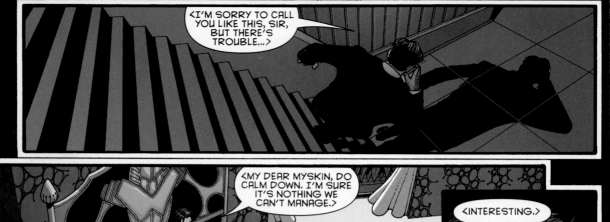

&lt;I'M SORRY TO CALL YOU LIKE THIS, SIR, BUT THERE'S TROUBLE...&gt;

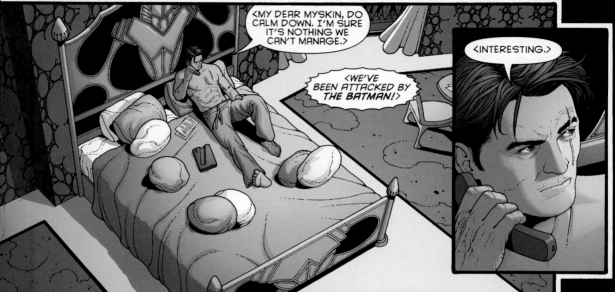

&lt;MY DEAR MYSKIN, DO CALM DOWN. I'M SURE IT'S NOTHING WE CAN'T MANAGE.&gt;

&lt;WE'VE BEEN ATTACKED BY *THE BATMAN!*&gt;

&lt;INTERESTING.&gt;

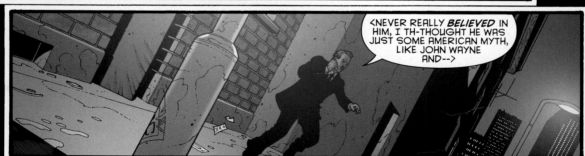

&lt;NEVER REALLY *BELIEVED* IN HIM, I TH-THOUGHT HE WAS JUST SOME AMERICAN MYTH, LIKE JOHN WAYNE AND--&gt;

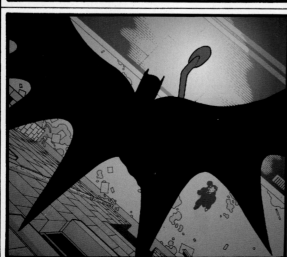

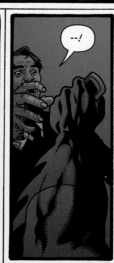

--!

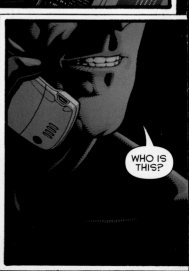

WHO IS THIS?

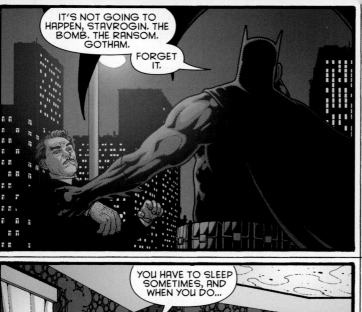

IT'S NOT GOING TO HAPPEN, STAVROGIN. THE BOMB. THE RANSOM. GOTHAM.

FORGET IT.

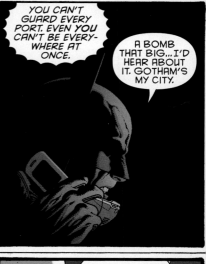

YOU CAN'T GUARD EVERY PORT. EVEN YOU CAN'T BE EVERY-WHERE AT ONCE.

A BOMB THAT BIG...I'D HEAR ABOUT IT. GOTHAM'S MY CITY.

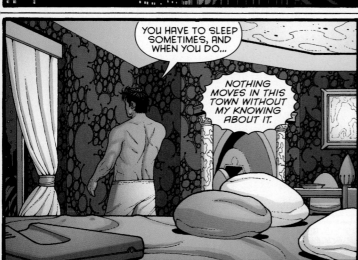

YOU HAVE TO SLEEP SOMETIMES, AND WHEN YOU DO...

NOTHING MOVES IN THIS TOWN WITHOUT MY KNOWING ABOUT IT.

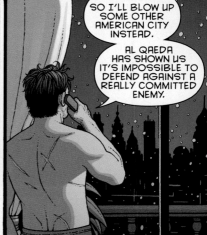

SO I'LL BLOW UP SOME OTHER AMERICAN CITY INSTEAD.

AL QAEDA HAS SHOWN US IT'S IMPOSSIBLE TO DEFEND AGAINST A REALLY COMMITTED ENEMY.

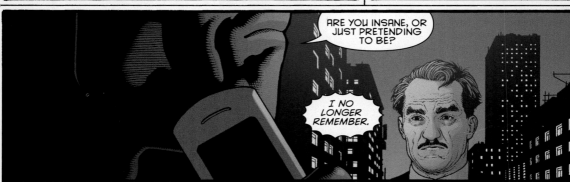

ARE YOU INSANE, OR JUST PRETENDING TO BE?

I NO LONGER REMEMBER.

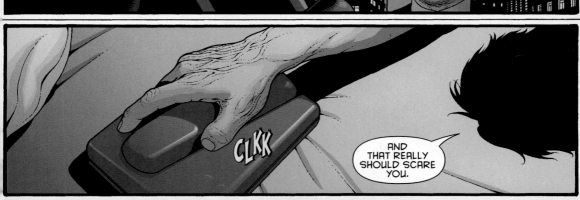

CLKK

AND THAT REALLY SHOULD SCARE YOU.

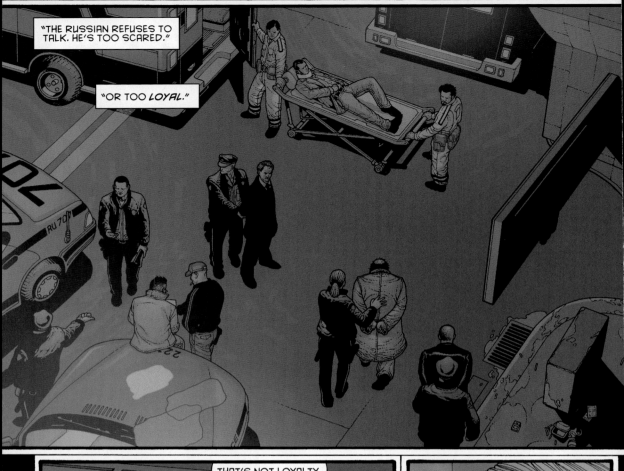

"THE RUSSIAN REFUSES TO TALK. HE'S TOO SCARED."

"OR TOO *LOYAL*."

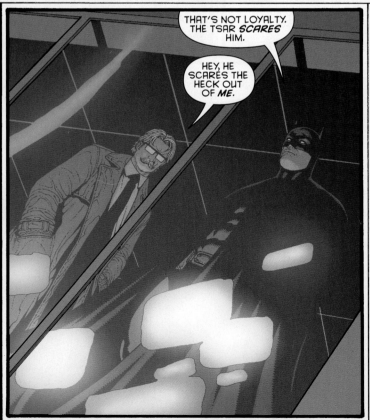

THAT'S NOT LOYALTY. THE TSAR *SCARES* HIM.

HEY, HE SCARES THE HECK OUT OF *ME*.

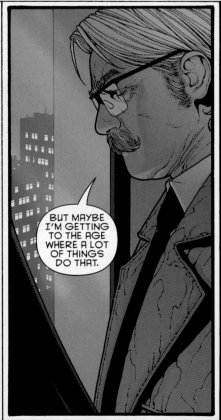

BUT MAYBE I'M GETTING TO THE AGE WHERE A LOT OF THINGS DO THAT.

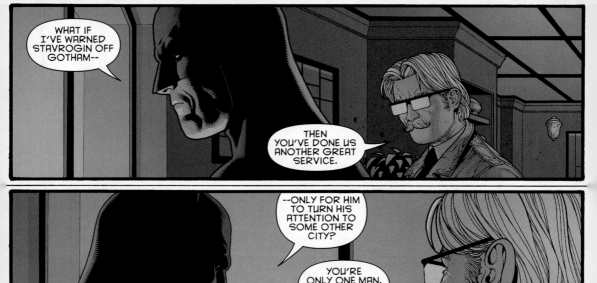

WHAT IF I'VE WARNED STAVROGIN OFF GOTHAM--

THEN YOU'VE DONE US ANOTHER GREAT SERVICE.

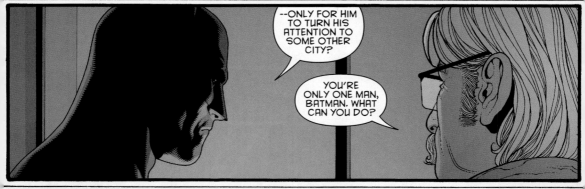

--ONLY FOR HIM TO TURN HIS ATTENTION TO SOME OTHER CITY?

YOU'RE ONLY ONE MAN, BATMAN. WHAT CAN YOU DO?

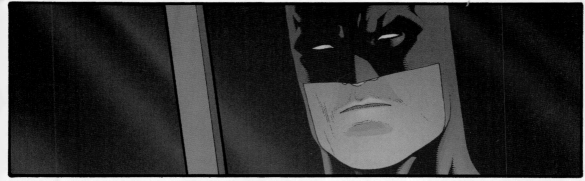

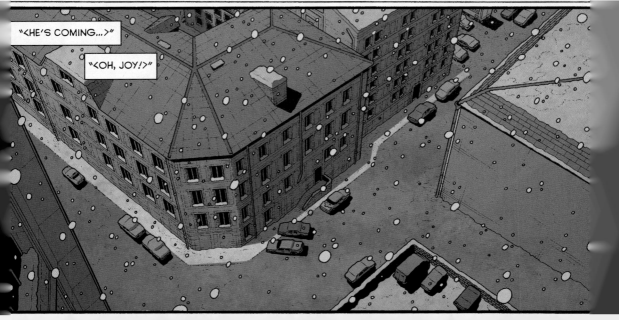

"‹HE'S COMING...›"

"‹OH, JOY!›"

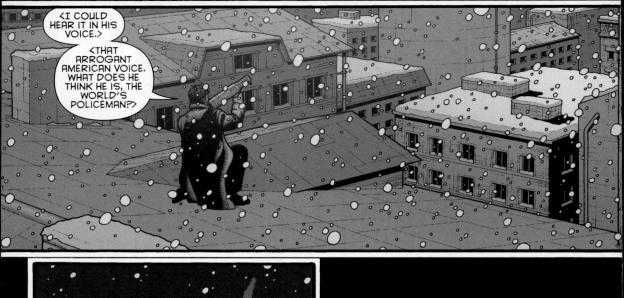

<I COULD HEAR IT IN HIS VOICE.>

<THAT ARROGANT AMERICAN VOICE. WHAT DOES HE THINK HE IS, THE WORLD'S POLICEMAN?>

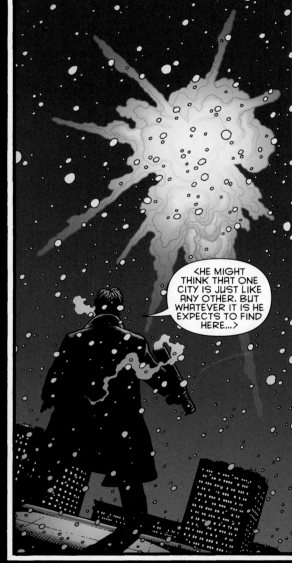

<HE MIGHT THINK THAT ONE CITY IS JUST LIKE ANY OTHER. BUT WHATEVER IT IS HE EXPECTS TO FIND HERE...>

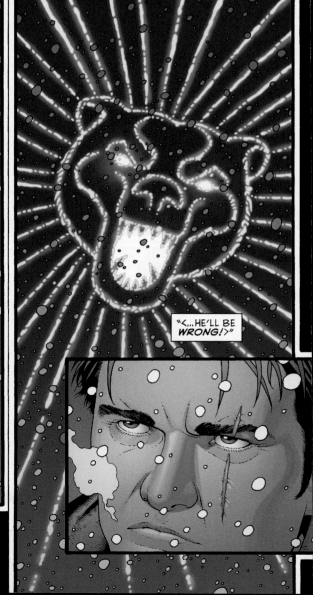

"<...HE'LL BE WRONG!>"

Cover by Guillem March

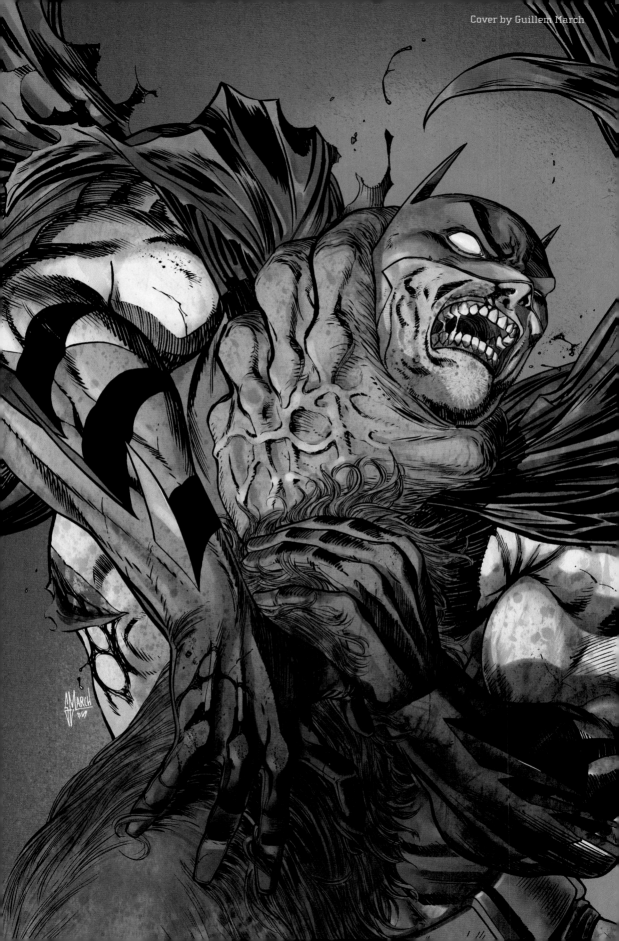

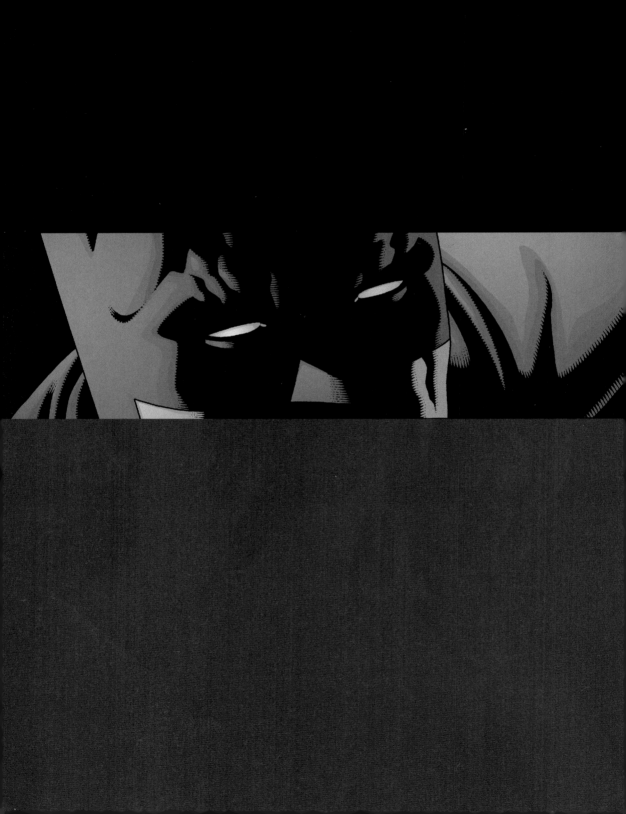

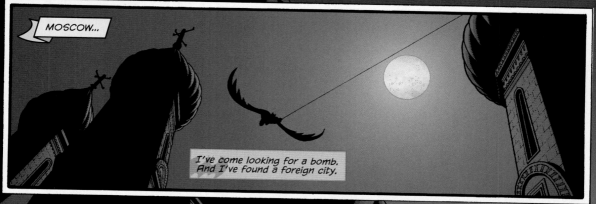

MOSCOW...

I've come looking for a bomb. And I've found a foreign city.

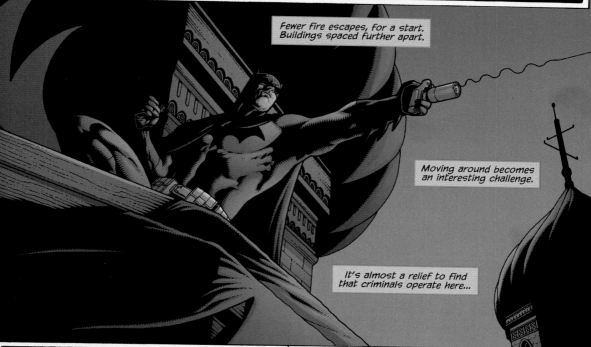

Fewer fire escapes, for a start. Buildings spaced further apart.

Moving around becomes an interesting challenge.

It's almost a relief to find that criminals operate here...

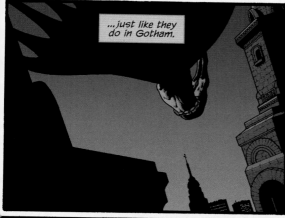

...just like they do in Gotham.

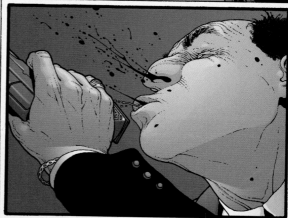

# THE BAT AND THE BEAST

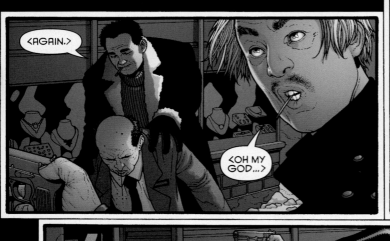

<AGAIN.>

<OH MY GOD...>

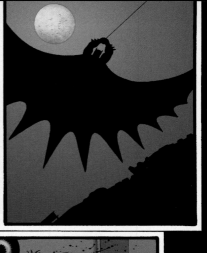

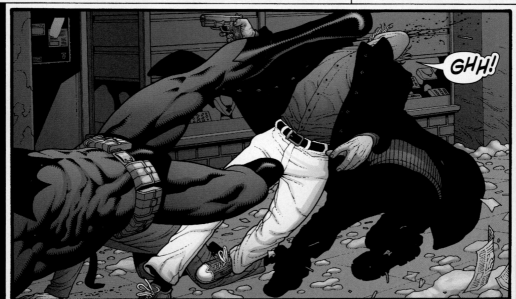

GHH!

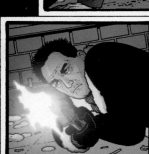

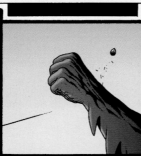

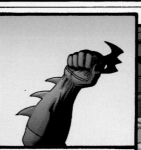

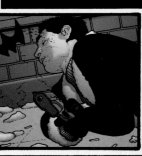

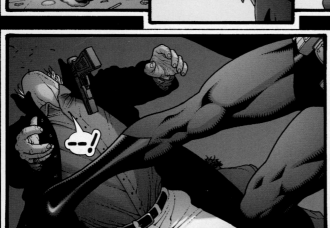

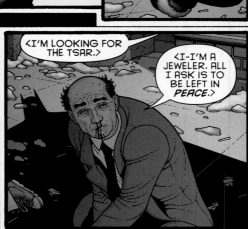

<I'M LOOKING FOR THE TSAR.>

<I-I'M A JEWELER. ALL I ASK IS TO BE LEFT IN PEACE.>

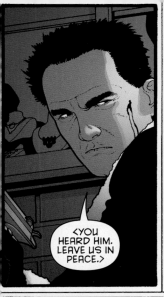

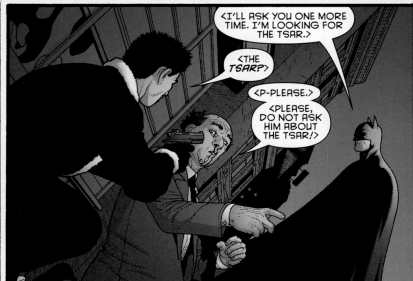

&lt;I'LL ASK YOU ONE MORE TIME. I'M LOOKING FOR THE TSAR.&gt;

&lt;THE *TSAR?*&gt;

&lt;P-PLEASE.&gt;

&lt;PLEASE, DO NOT ASK HIM ABOUT THE TSAR!&gt;

&lt;YOU HEARD HIM. LEAVE US IN PEACE.&gt;

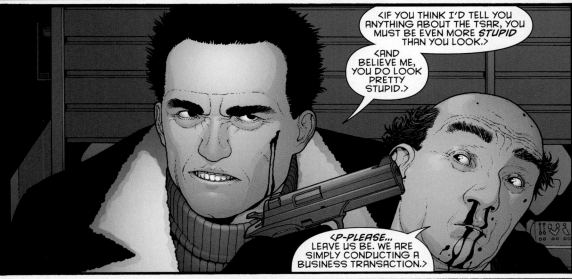

&lt;IF YOU THINK I'D TELL YOU ANYTHING ABOUT THE TSAR, YOU MUST BE EVEN MORE *STUPID* THAN YOU LOOK.&gt;

&lt;AND BELIEVE ME, YOU DO LOOK PRETTY STUPID.&gt;

&lt;P-PLEASE... LEAVE US BE. WE ARE SIMPLY CONDUCTING A BUSINESS TRANSACTION.&gt;

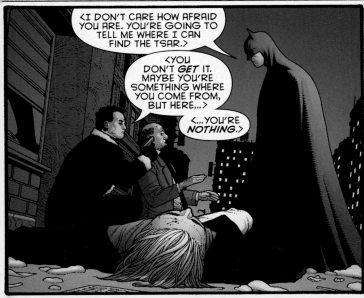

&lt;I DON'T CARE HOW AFRAID YOU ARE. YOU'RE GOING TO TELL ME WHERE I CAN FIND THE TSAR.&gt;

&lt;YOU DON'T *GET* IT. MAYBE YOU'RE SOMETHING WHERE YOU COME FROM, BUT HERE...&gt;

&lt;...YOU'RE *NOTHING.*&gt;

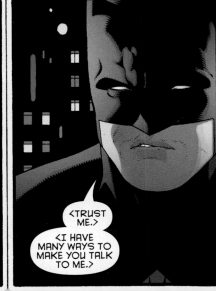

&lt;TRUST ME.&gt;

&lt;I HAVE MANY WAYS TO MAKE YOU TALK TO ME.&gt;

<I MIGHT AS WELL KILL MYSELF AS TALK TO YOU ABOUT THE TSAR.>
He's bluffing. Feigning craziness.
<HE MEANS IT!>
NO!
BAAAM
<I TOLD YOU HE MEANT IT.>
<BY THE WAY, THE OTHER ONE'S GETTING AWAY.>
It's insane.
I hadn't even pushed him.
Hadn't even hung him by his feet from a high building.

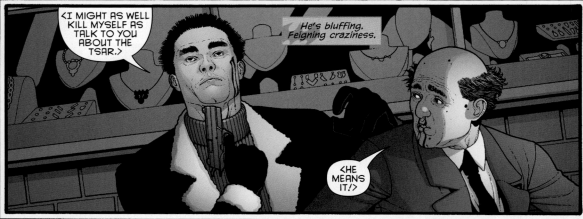

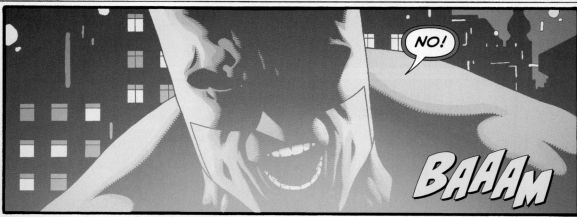

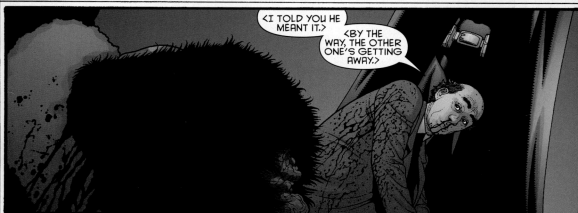

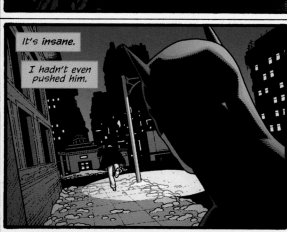

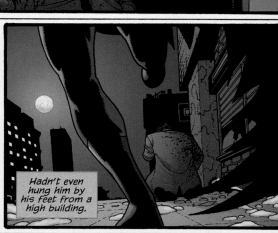

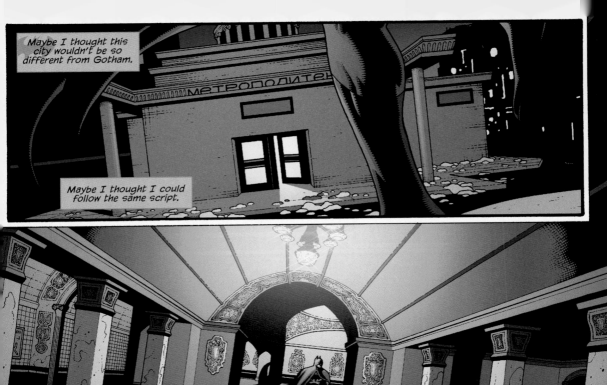

Maybe I thought this city wouldn't be so different from Gotham.

Maybe I thought I could follow the same script.

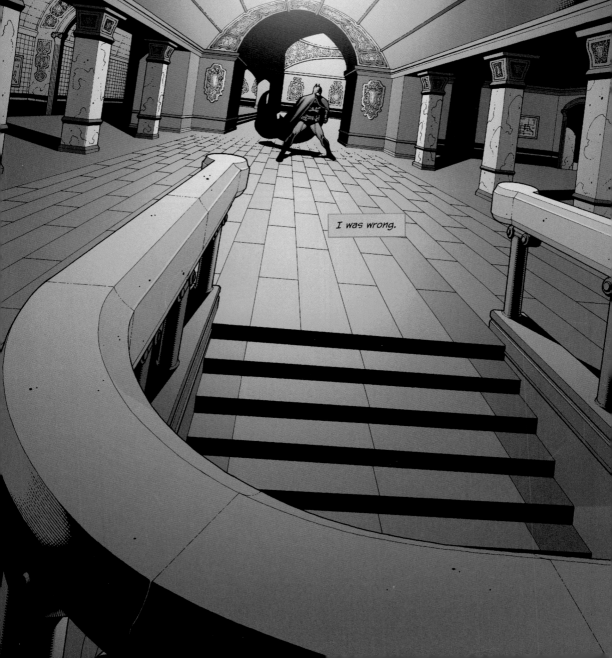

I was wrong.

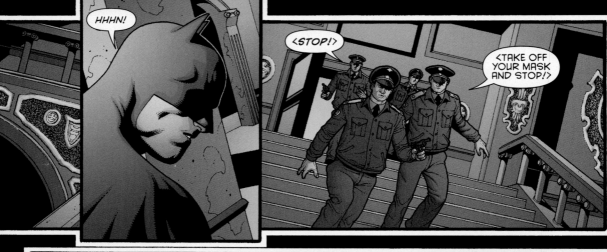

HHHN!

&lt;STOP!&gt;

&lt;TAKE OFF YOUR MASK AND STOP!&gt;

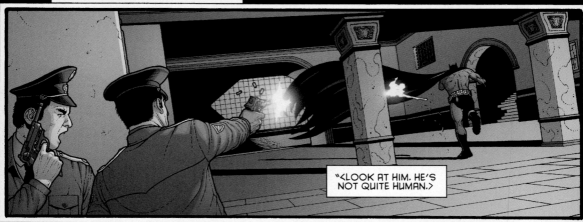

"&lt;LOOK AT HIM. HE'S NOT QUITE HUMAN.&gt;"

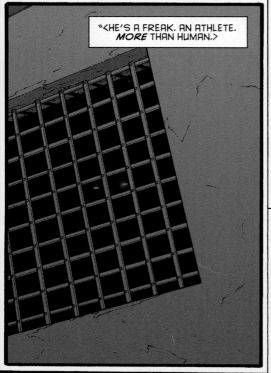

"&lt;HE'S A FREAK. AN ATHLETE. *MORE* THAN HUMAN.&gt;"

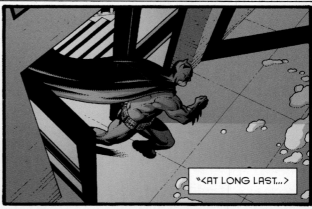

"&lt;AT LONG LAST...&gt;"

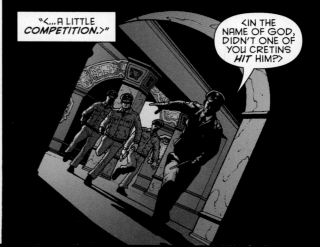

"&lt;...A LITTLE *COMPETITION*.&gt;"

&lt;IN THE NAME OF GOD, DIDN'T ONE OF YOU CRETINS *HIT* HIM?&gt;

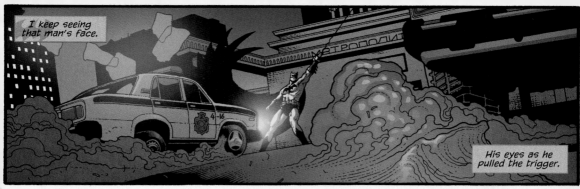

I keep seeing that man's face.

His eyes as he pulled the trigger.

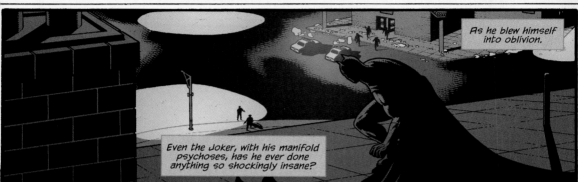

As he blew himself into oblivion.

Even the Joker, with his manifold psychoses, has he ever done anything so shockingly insane?

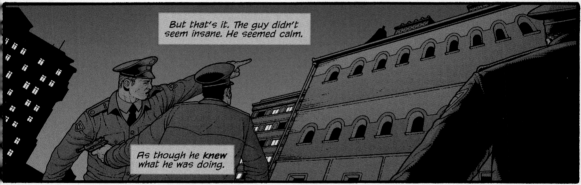

But that's it. The guy didn't seem insane. He seemed calm.

As though he knew what he was doing.

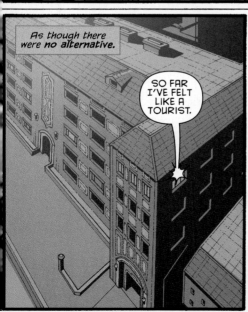

As though there were no alternative.

SO FAR I'VE FELT LIKE A TOURIST.

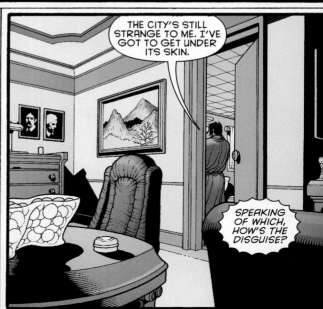

THE CITY'S STILL STRANGE TO ME. I'VE GOT TO GET UNDER ITS SKIN.

SPEAKING OF WHICH, HOW'S THE DISGUISE?

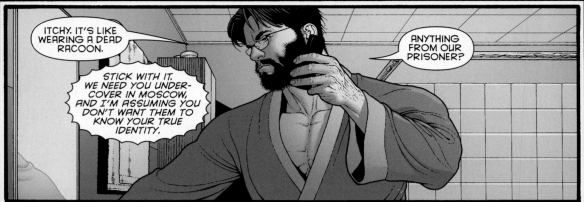

ITCHY. IT'S LIKE WEARING A DEAD RACOON.

ANYTHING FROM OUR PRISONER?

STICK WITH IT. WE NEED YOU UNDER-COVER IN MOSCOW, AND I'M ASSUMING YOU DON'T WANT THEM TO KNOW YOUR TRUE IDENTITY.

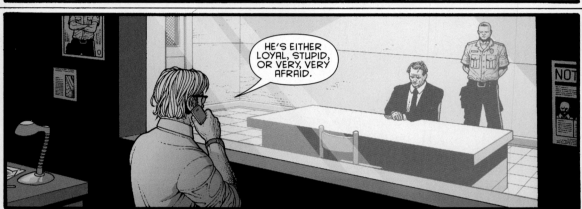

HE'S EITHER LOYAL, STUPID, OR VERY, VERY AFRAID.

NOT

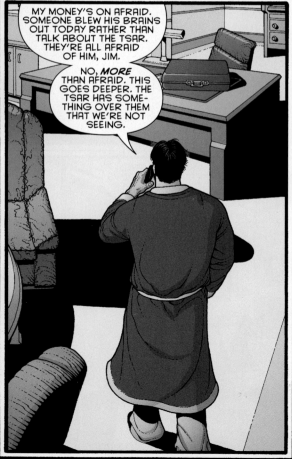

MY MONEY'S ON AFRAID. SOMEONE BLEW HIS BRAINS OUT TODAY RATHER THAN TALK ABOUT THE TSAR. THEY'RE ALL AFRAID OF HIM, JIM.

NO, MORE THAN AFRAID. THIS GOES DEEPER. THE TSAR HAS SOME-THING OVER THEM THAT WE'RE NOT SEEING.

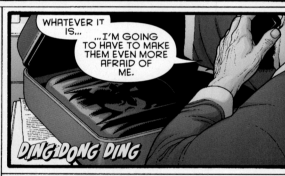

WHATEVER IT IS...

...I'M GOING TO HAVE TO MAKE THEM EVEN MORE AFRAID OF ME.

DING DONG DING

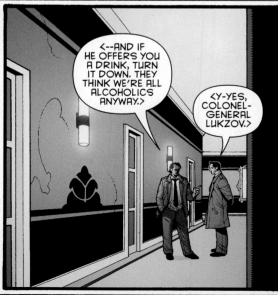

<--AND IF HE OFFERS YOU A DRINK, TURN IT DOWN. THEY THINK WE'RE ALL ALCOHOLICS ANYWAY.>

<Y-YES, COLONEL-GENERAL LUKZOV.>

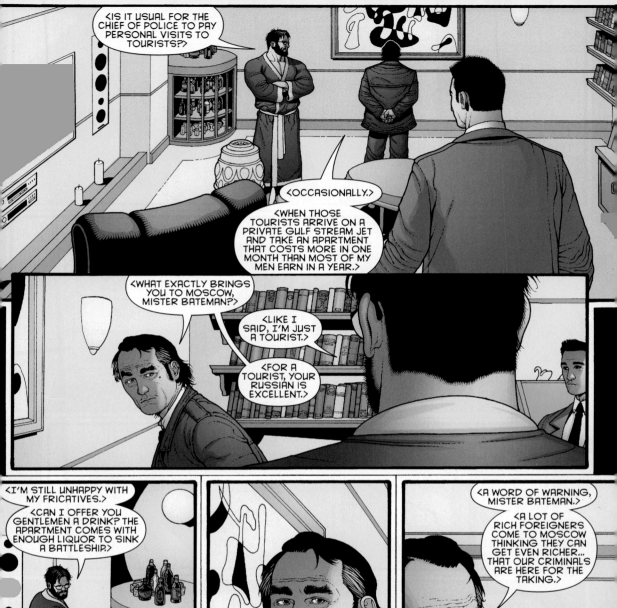

‹IS IT USUAL FOR THE CHIEF OF POLICE TO PAY PERSONAL VISITS TO TOURISTS?›

‹OCCASIONALLY.›

‹WHEN THOSE TOURISTS ARRIVE ON A PRIVATE GULF STREAM JET AND TAKE AN APARTMENT THAT COSTS MORE IN ONE MONTH THAN MOST OF MY MEN EARN IN A YEAR.›

‹WHAT EXACTLY BRINGS YOU TO MOSCOW, MISTER BATEMAN?›

‹LIKE I SAID, I'M JUST A TOURIST.›

‹FOR A TOURIST, YOUR RUSSIAN IS EXCELLENT.›

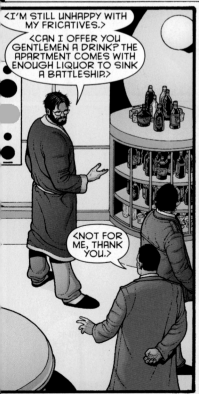

‹I'M STILL UNHAPPY WITH MY FRICATIVES.›

‹CAN I OFFER YOU GENTLEMEN A DRINK? THE APARTMENT COMES WITH ENOUGH LIQUOR TO SINK A BATTLESHIP.›

‹NOT FOR ME, THANK YOU.›

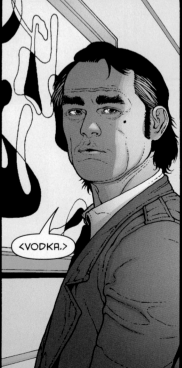

‹VODKA.›

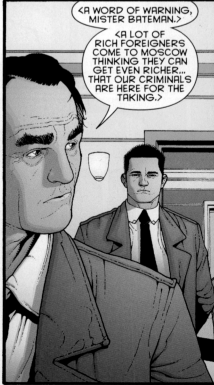

‹A WORD OF WARNING, MISTER BATEMAN.›

‹A LOT OF RICH FOREIGNERS COME TO MOSCOW THINKING THEY CAN GET EVEN RICHER... THAT OUR CRIMINALS ARE HERE FOR THE TAKING.›

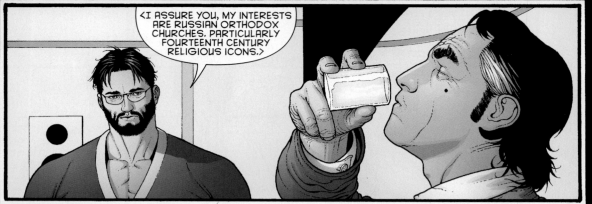

<I ASSURE YOU, MY INTERESTS ARE RUSSIAN ORTHODOX CHURCHES. PARTICULARLY FOURTEENTH CENTURY RELIGIOUS ICONS.>

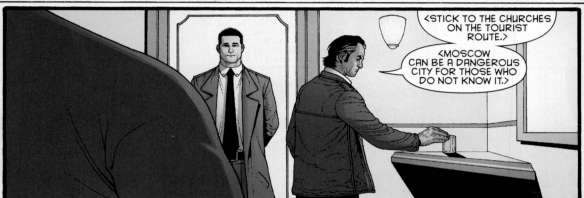

<STICK TO THE CHURCHES ON THE TOURIST ROUTE.>

<MOSCOW CAN BE A DANGEROUS CITY FOR THOSE WHO DO NOT KNOW IT.>

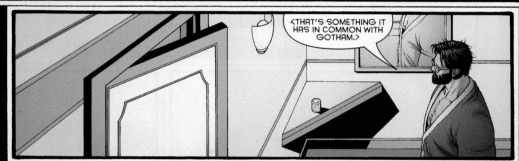

<THAT'S SOMETHING IT HAS IN COMMON WITH GOTHAM.>

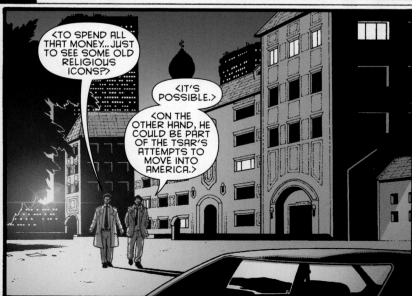

<TO SPEND ALL THAT MONEY... JUST TO SEE SOME OLD RELIGIOUS ICONS?>

<IT'S POSSIBLE.>

<ON THE OTHER HAND, HE COULD BE PART OF THE TSAR'S ATTEMPTS TO MOVE INTO AMERICA.>

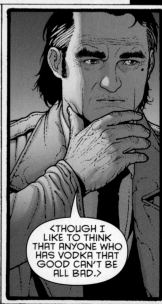

<THOUGH I LIKE TO THINK THAT ANYONE WHO HAS VODKA THAT GOOD CAN'T BE ALL BAD.>

<TH-THIS IS NOT GOOD. NOT GOOD!>
<WHERE'S SASHA?>
<S-SOMETHING HIT HIM. FORGET HIM!>
<WAS IT THE BEAR?>
<NO, THIS WAS-->
<OH GOD.>
<NIKI, *LOOK!*>
<IT'S A BIG *BAT*. LIKE THE AMERICAN BAT MAN-->
<--BUT *BIGGER*.>
<RUSSIAN.>
*I see that look on their faces.*

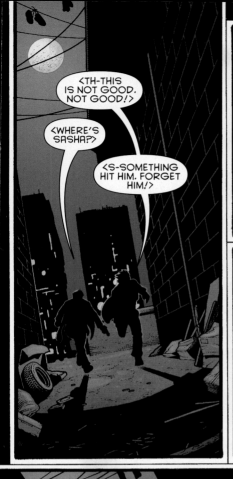

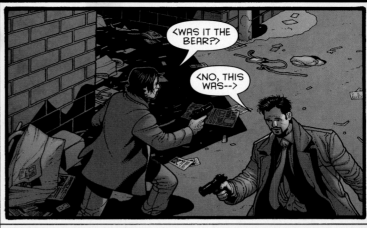

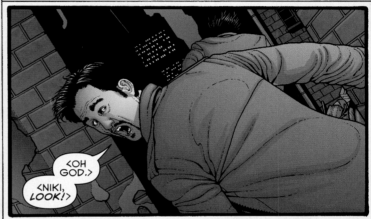

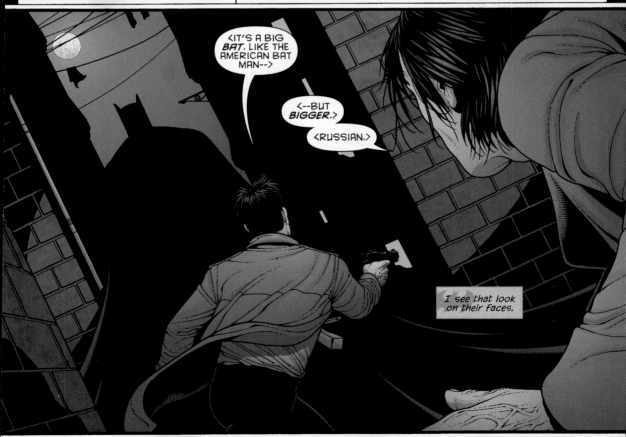

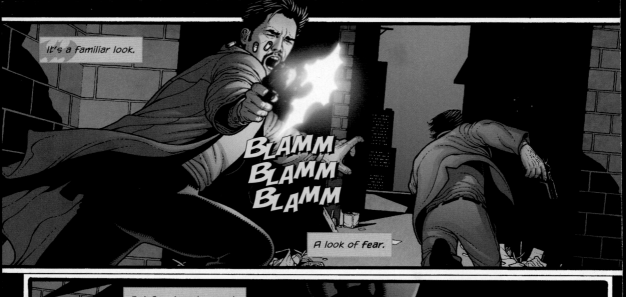

It's a familiar look.

BLAMM
BLAMM
BLAMM

A look of fear.

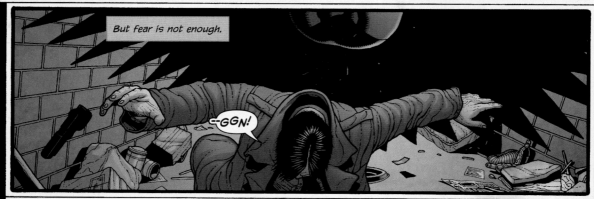

But fear is not enough.

--GGN!

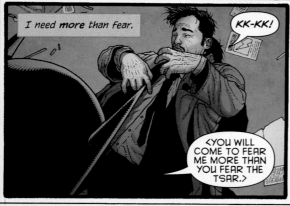

I need *more* than fear.

KK-KK!

<YOU WILL COME TO FEAR ME MORE THAN YOU FEAR THE TSAR.>

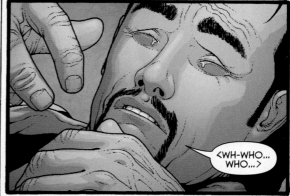

<WH-WHO... WHO...>

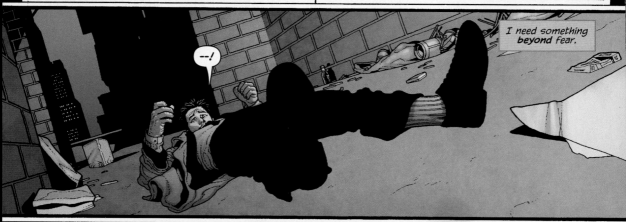

--!

I need something *beyond* fear.

<THAT'S WHAT HE SAID?>
<Y-YES, SIR. HE'S A BAT MAN... BUT MORE BAT THAN MAN.>
<ALL RIGHT, NIKI. YOU CAN GO NOW.>
<YOU KNOW, DON'T YOU, FYODOR? THEY ***WANT*** FEAR.>
<FEAR MAKES THEM FEEL ***ALIVE***. IT'S LIKE A DRUG. STALIN KNEW THIS. STALIN WAS THE ULTIMATE DEALER IN FEAR.>
<LET ***ME*** GO AFTER HIM.>
<SOON, FYODOR.>
<A MAN WHO'S NOT A MAN. THAT'S... THAT'S VERY ***INTERESTING***.>
<HE'S HERE TO ***HURT*** US. HE IS AN INVADER.>
<NOT THE FIRST MOSCOW HAS SUFFERED...>

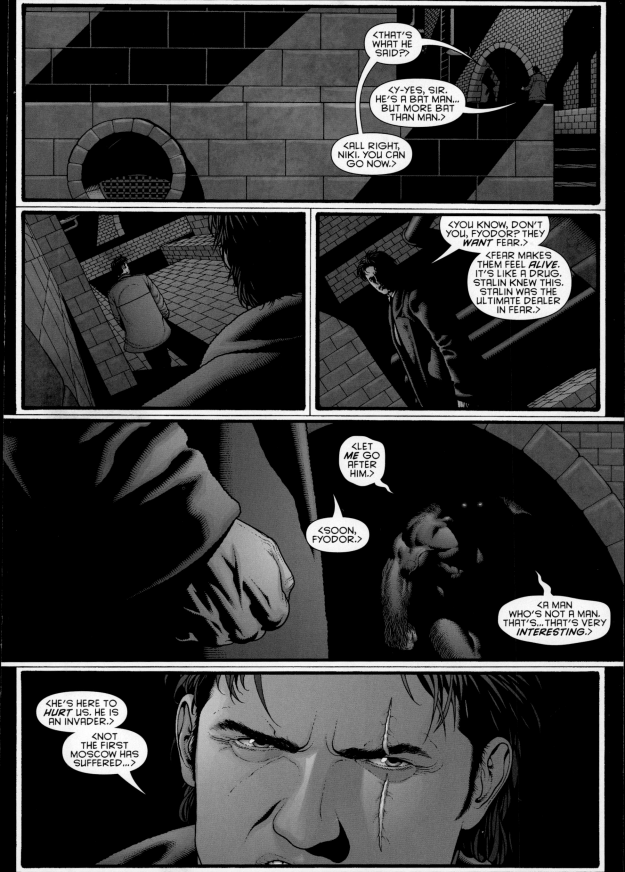

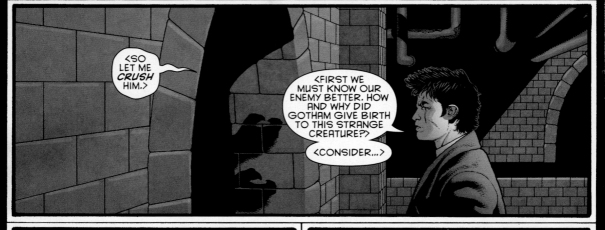

&lt;SO LET ME *CRUSH* HIM.&gt;

&lt;FIRST WE MUST KNOW OUR ENEMY BETTER. HOW AND WHY DID GOTHAM GIVE BIRTH TO THIS STRANGE CREATURE?&gt;

&lt;CONSIDER...&gt;

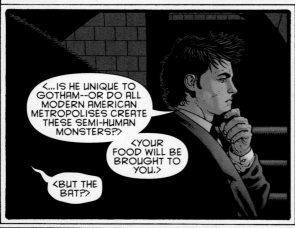

&lt;...IS HE UNIQUE TO GOTHAM--OR DO ALL MODERN AMERICAN METROPOLISES CREATE THESE SEMI-HUMAN MONSTERS?&gt;

&lt;YOUR FOOD WILL BE BROUGHT TO YOU.&gt;

&lt;BUT THE BAT?&gt;

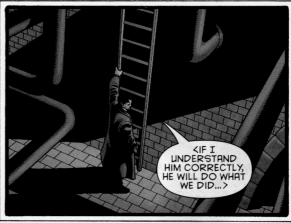

&lt;IF I UNDERSTAND HIM CORRECTLY, HE WILL DO WHAT WE DID...&gt;

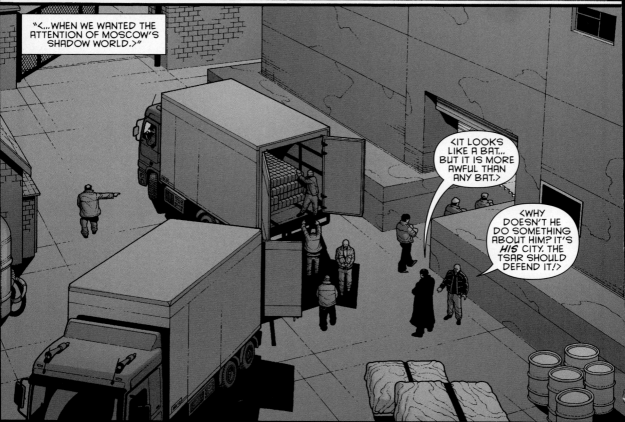

"&lt;...WHEN WE WANTED THE ATTENTION OF MOSCOW'S SHADOW WORLD.&gt;"

&lt;IT LOOKS LIKE A BAT... BUT IT IS MORE AWFUL THAN ANY BAT.&gt;

&lt;WHY DOESN'T HE DO SOMETHING ABOUT HIM? IT'S *HIS* CITY. THE TSAR SHOULD DEFEND IT!&gt;

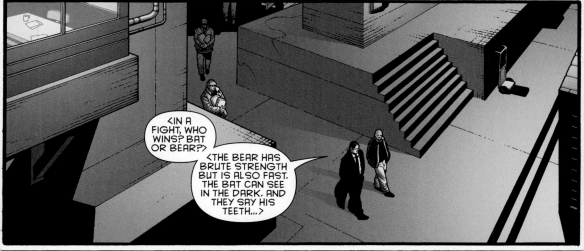

<IN A FIGHT, WHO WINS? BAT OR BEAR?>

<THE BEAR HAS BRUTE STRENGTH BUT IS ALSO FAST. THE BAT CAN SEE IN THE DARK. AND THEY SAY HIS TEETH...>

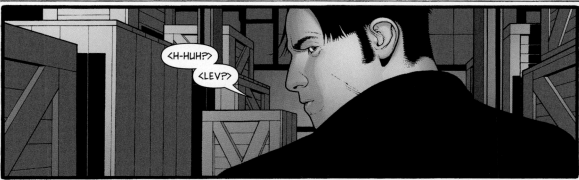

<H-HUH?>

<LEV?>

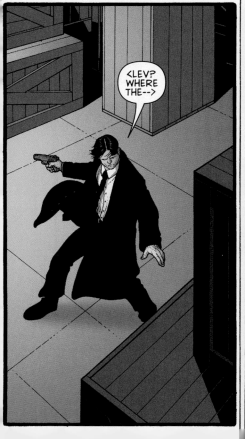

<LEV? WHERE THE-->

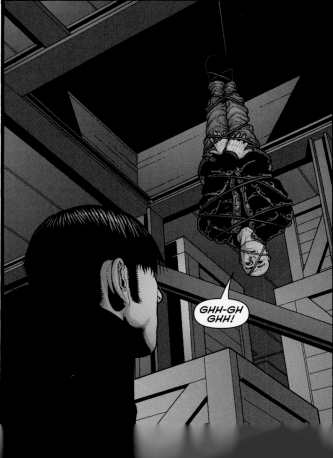

GHH-GH GHH!

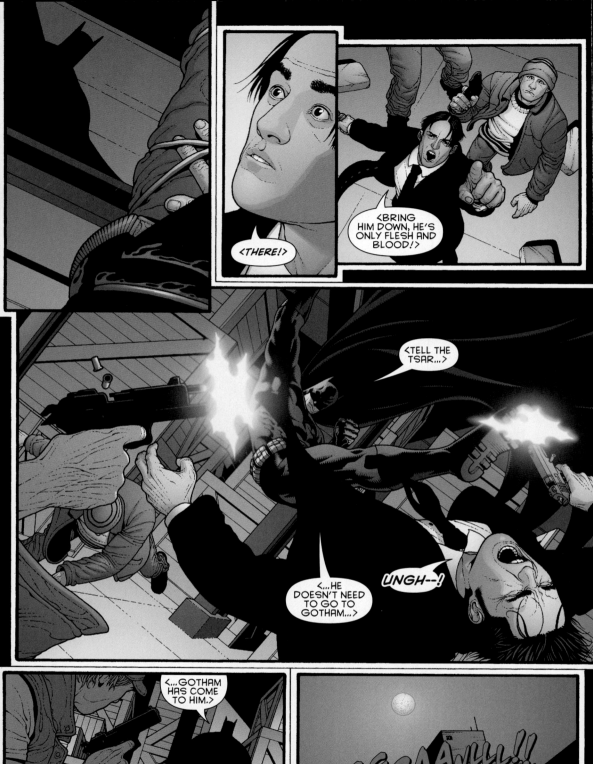

<THERE!>

<BRING HIM DOWN, HE'S ONLY FLESH AND BLOOD!>

<TELL THE TSAR...>

<...HE DOESN'T NEED TO GO TO GOTHAM...>

UNGH--!

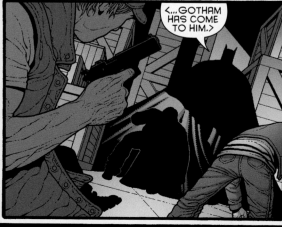

<...GOTHAM HAS COME TO HIM.>

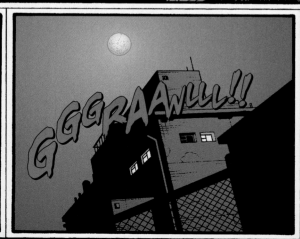

GGGRAAWLLL!!

<TH-THE BEAR!>
<IT'S THE BEAR!>
The Bear?
Suddenly.
Suddenly a man's suicide starts to make a little more sense.
GRAWWWLLL!
<NOW WE SEE THE BAT GET HIS WINGS TORN OFF.>
<THIS IS THE TSAR'S CITY.>
<YOU'RE NOT A BAT.>
<AND YOU'RE NOT A BEAR.>
<WHY HAVE YOU COME HERE TO HURT US?>

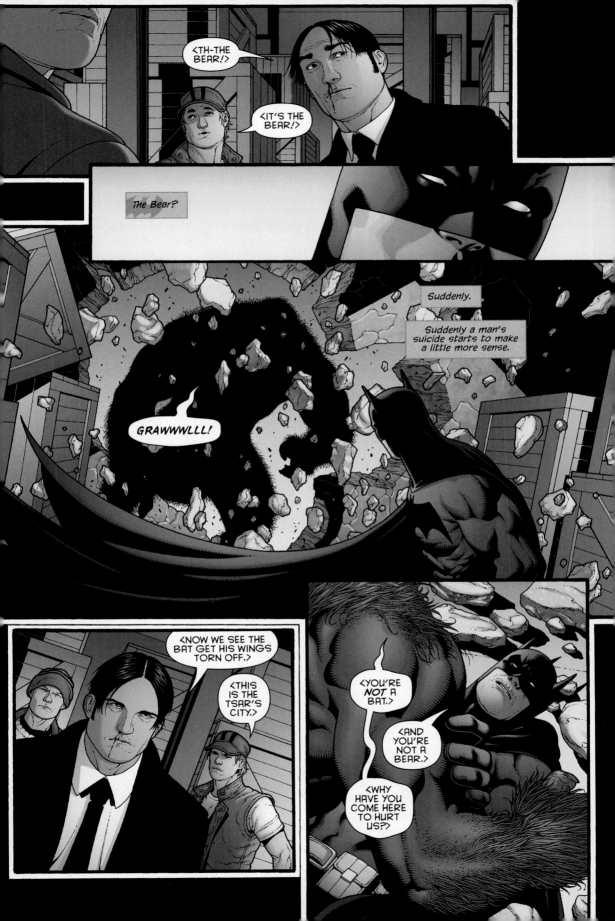

<I DON'T WANT TO HURT ANYONE.>
<NOT IF I CAN AVOID IT.>
--!
<THE TSAR IS AN EVIL CRIMINAL-->
<NO! THE TSAR TOLD ME-->
<HE'S A MANIAC.>
<--HE SAID YOU WANT TO...HURT US.>
<HE'S LYING. HE'S-->
<THE BAT'S FIGHTING BACK! HE'S TOUGH.>
<HE CAN'T LAST LONG. NOT AGAINST THE BEAR.>
Yes, I understand the look in the suicide's eyes.
Understand what lies beyond fear.
KR--SSH

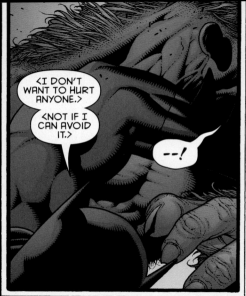

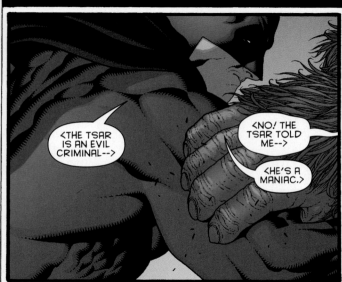

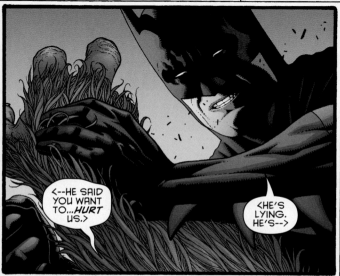

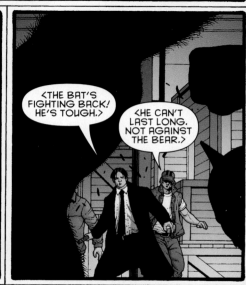

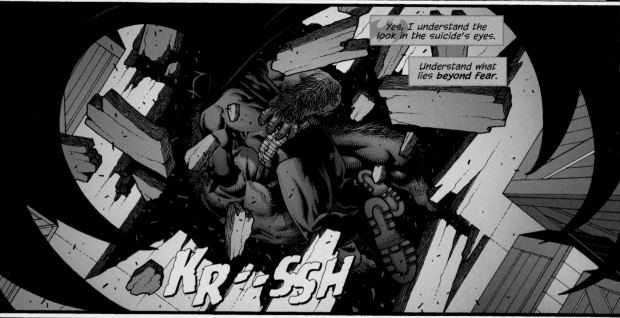

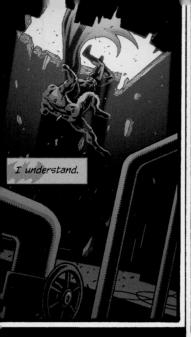

I understand.

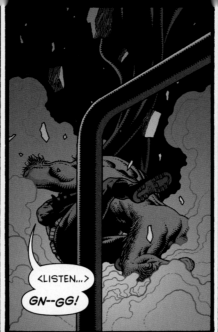

<LISTEN...>

GN--GG!

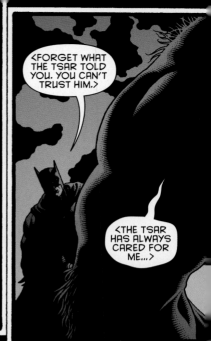

<FORGET WHAT THE TSAR TOLD YOU. YOU CAN'T TRUST HIM.>

<THE TSAR HAS ALWAYS CARED FOR ME...>

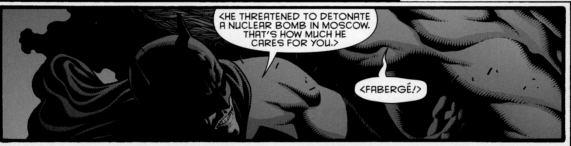

<HE THREATENED TO DETONATE A NUCLEAR BOMB IN MOSCOW. THAT'S HOW MUCH HE CARES FOR YOU.>

<FABERGÉ!>

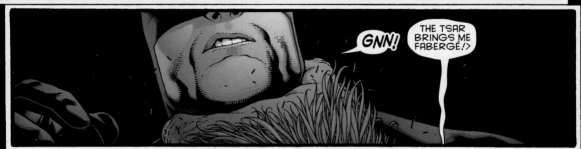

GNN!

THE TSAR BRINGS ME FABERGÉ!>

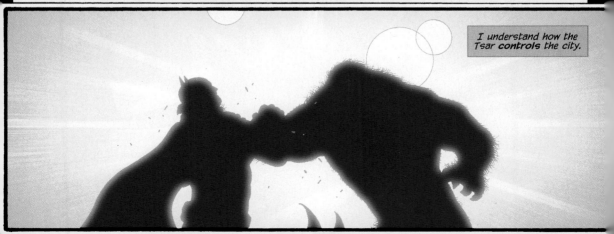

I understand how the Tsar **controls** the city.

But understanding is only **part** of the problem.
--!

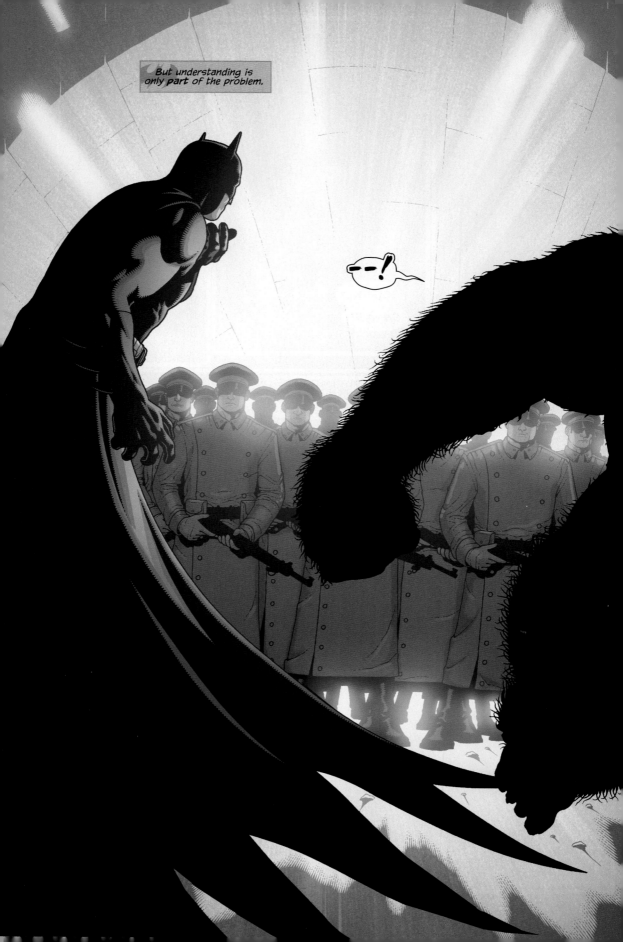

<IF YOU SEE THAT DOLT OUTSIDE FALL ASLEEP CALL ME IMMEDIATELY. YOU PROMISE ME, ANNA?>
<JUST DON'T FORGET TO SAY GOODBYE TO SVETI BEFORE YOU GO.>
<'NIGHT, BABUSHKA. STUDYING HARD?>
<WHY DID THEY MAKE ENGLISH SO DIFFICULT TO PRONOUNCE?>
<JUST KEEP PRACTICING THE FRICATIVES.>
<YOU LOOK WORRIED, DMITRI. WHAT IS IT?>
<THERE'S SOMETHING IN THE AIR. A CHANGE IN THE WEATHER MAYBE.>
"<YOU KNOW HOW CHANGE SCARES ME.>"

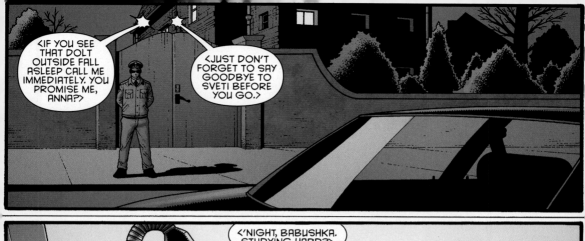

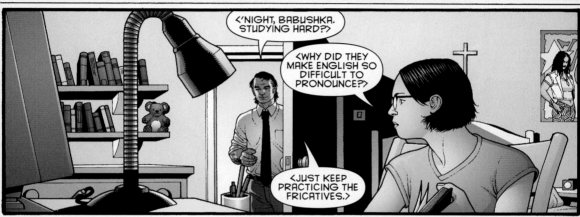

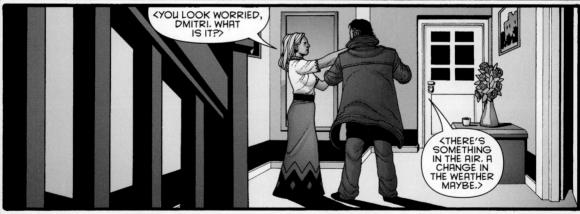

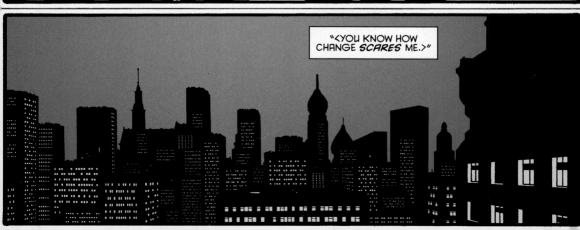

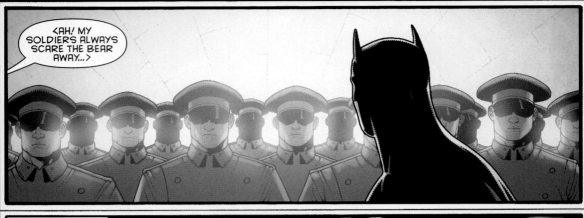

&lt;AH! MY SOLDIERS ALWAYS SCARE THE BEAR AWAY...&gt;

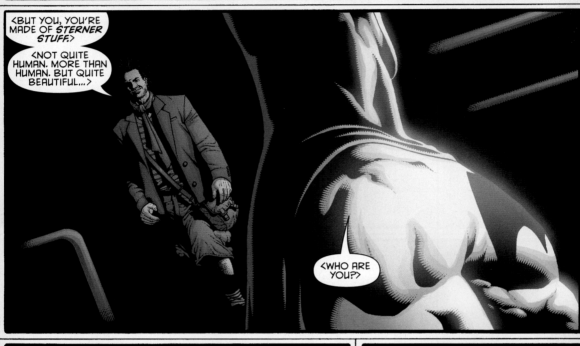

&lt;BUT YOU, YOU'RE MADE OF *STERNER STUFF*.&gt;

&lt;NOT QUITE HUMAN. MORE THAN HUMAN. BUT QUITE BEAUTIFUL...&gt;

&lt;WHO ARE YOU?&gt;

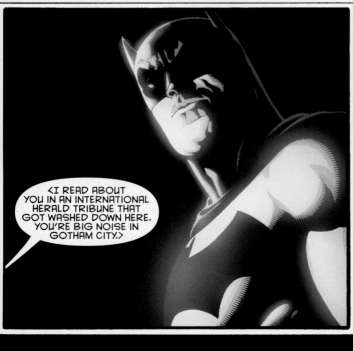

&lt;I READ ABOUT YOU IN AN INTERNATIONAL HERALD TRIBUNE THAT GOT WASHED DOWN HERE. YOU'RE BIG NOISE IN GOTHAM CITY.&gt;

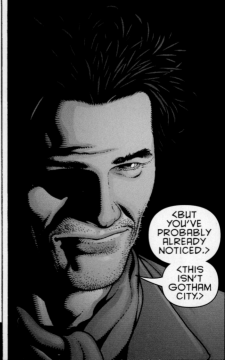

&lt;BUT YOU'VE PROBABLY ALREADY NOTICED.&gt;

&lt;THIS ISN'T GOTHAM CITY.&gt;

Cover by Jock

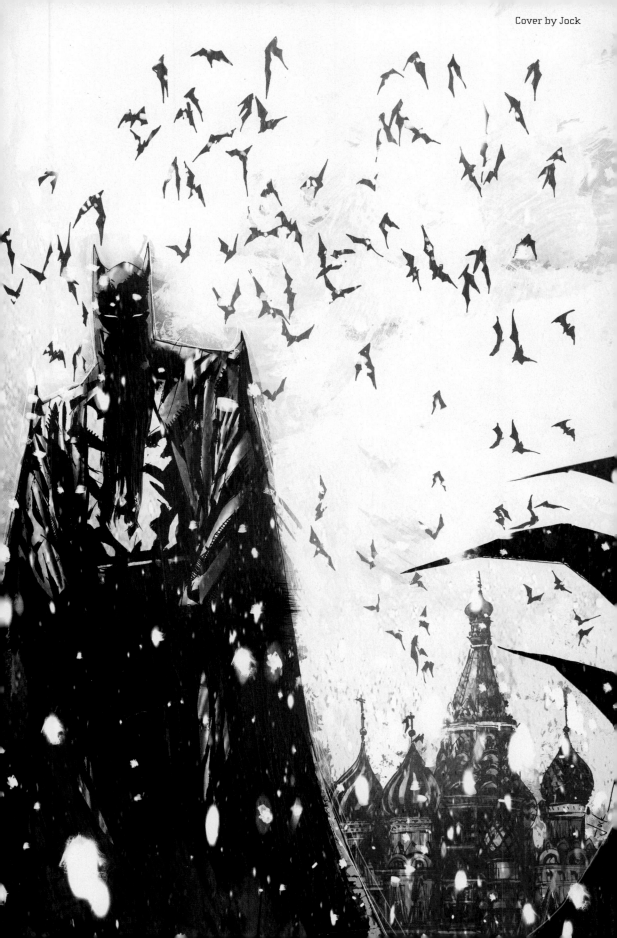

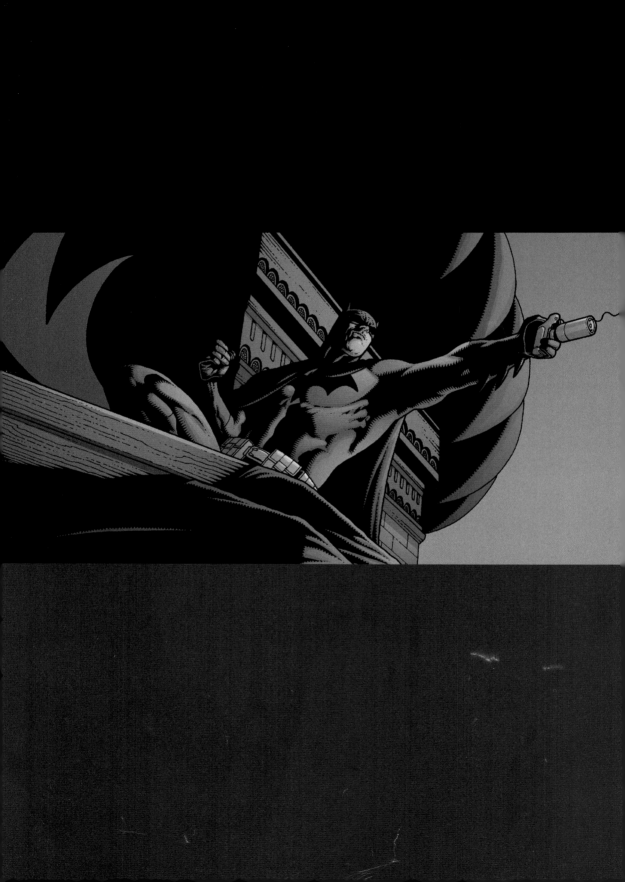

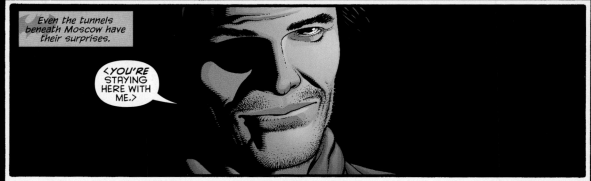

Even the tunnels beneath Moscow have their surprises.

<YOU'RE STAYING HERE WITH ME.>

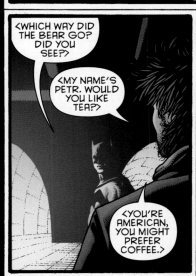

<WHICH WAY DID THE BEAR GO? DID YOU SEE?>

<MY NAME'S PETR. WOULD YOU LIKE TEA?>

<YOU'RE AMERICAN, YOU MIGHT PREFER COFFEE.>

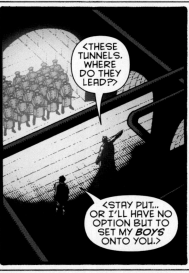

<THESE TUNNELS. WHERE DO THEY LEAD?>

<STAY PUT... OR I'LL HAVE NO OPTION BUT TO SET MY BOYS ONTO YOU.>

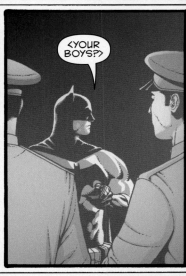

<YOUR BOYS?>

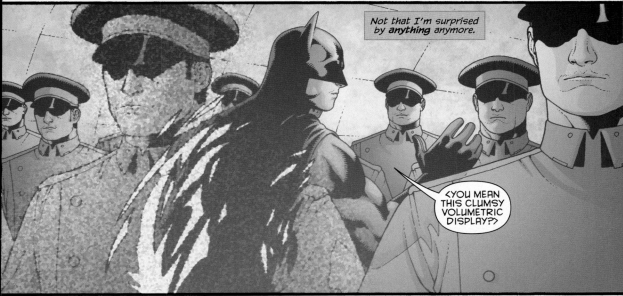

Not that I'm surprised by anything anymore.

<YOU MEAN THIS CLUMSY VOLUMETRIC DISPLAY?>

# THE BAT AND THE BEAST
## PART THREE

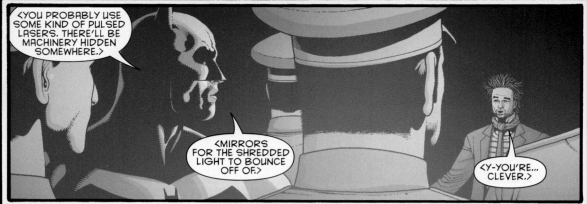

&lt;YOU PROBABLY USE SOME KIND OF PULSED LASERS. THERE'LL BE MACHINERY HIDDEN SOMEWHERE.&gt;

&lt;MIRRORS FOR THE SHREDDED LIGHT TO BOUNCE OFF OF.&gt;

&lt;Y-YOU'RE... CLEVER.&gt;

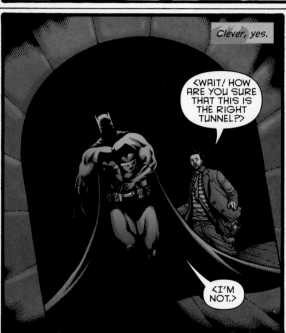

Clever, yes.

&lt;WAIT! HOW ARE YOU SURE THAT THIS IS THE RIGHT TUNNEL?&gt;

&lt;I'M NOT.&gt;

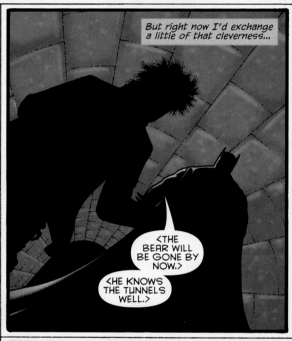

But right now I'd exchange a little of that cleverness...

&lt;THE BEAR WILL BE GONE BY NOW.&gt;

&lt;HE KNOWS THE TUNNELS WELL.&gt;

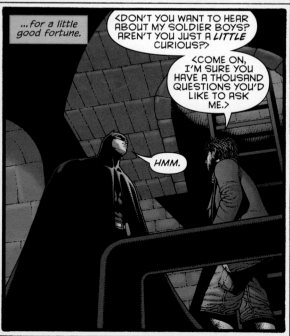

...for a little good fortune.

&lt;DON'T YOU WANT TO HEAR ABOUT MY SOLDIER BOYS? AREN'T YOU JUST A *LITTLE* CURIOUS?&gt;

&lt;COME ON, I'M SURE YOU HAVE A THOUSAND QUESTIONS YOU'D LIKE TO ASK ME.&gt;

HMM.

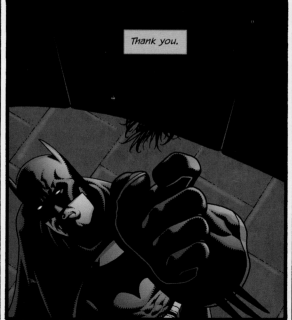

Thank you.

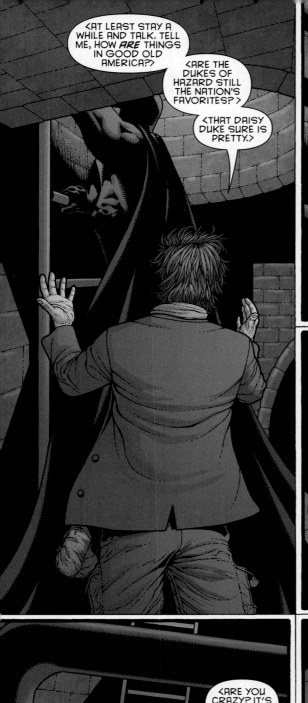

<AT LEAST STAY A WHILE AND TALK. TELL ME, HOW *ARE* THINGS IN GOOD OLD AMERICA?>

<ARE THE DUKES OF HAZARD STILL THE NATION'S FAVORITES?>

<THAT DAISY DUKE SURE IS PRETTY.>

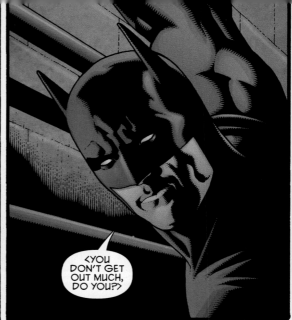

<YOU DON'T GET OUT MUCH, DO YOU?>

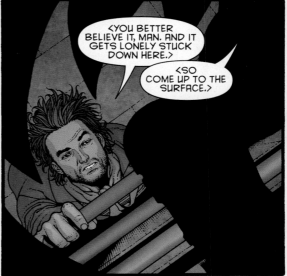

<YOU BETTER BELIEVE IT, MAN. AND IT GETS LONELY STUCK DOWN HERE.>

<SO COME UP TO THE SURFACE.>

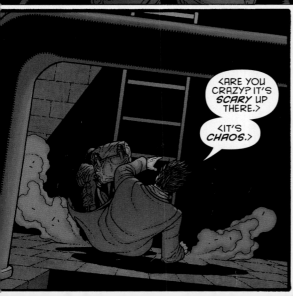

<ARE YOU CRAZY? IT'S *SCARY* UP THERE.>

<IT'S *CHAOS*.>

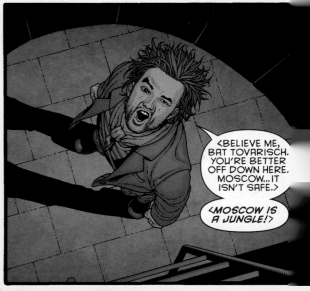

<BELIEVE ME, BAT TOVARISCH. YOU'RE BETTER OFF DOWN HERE. MOSCOW... IT ISN'T SAFE.>

<MOSCOW IS A JUNGLE!>

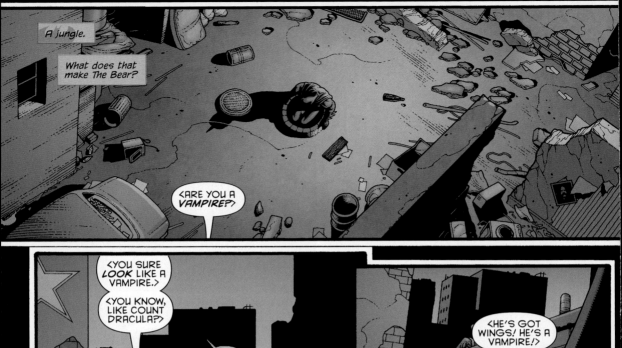

A jungle.

What does that make The Bear?

<ARE YOU A *VAMPIRE?*>

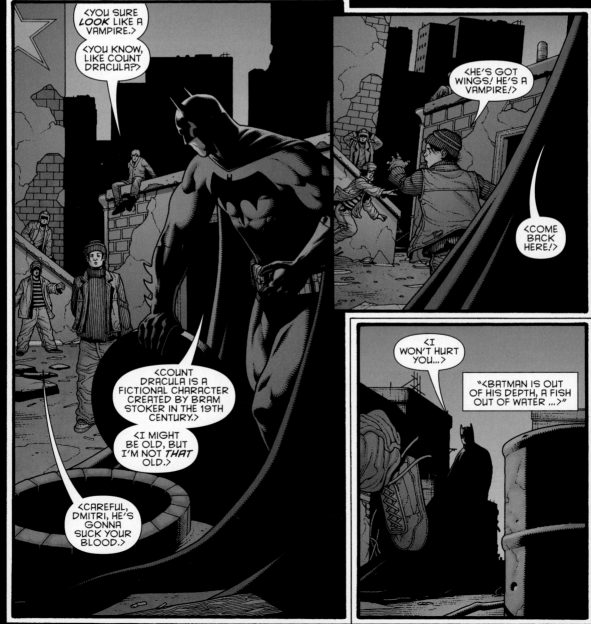

<YOU SURE *LOOK* LIKE A VAMPIRE.>

<YOU KNOW, LIKE COUNT DRACULA?>

<HE'S GOT WINGS! HE'S A VAMPIRE!>

<COME BACK HERE!>

<COUNT DRACULA IS A FICTIONAL CHARACTER CREATED BY BRAM STOKER IN THE 19TH CENTURY.>

<I MIGHT BE OLD, BUT I'M NOT *THAT* OLD.>

<CAREFUL, DMITRI, HE'S GONNA SUCK YOUR BLOOD.>

<I WON'T HURT YOU...>

"<BATMAN IS OUT OF HIS DEPTH, A FISH OUT OF WATER ...>"

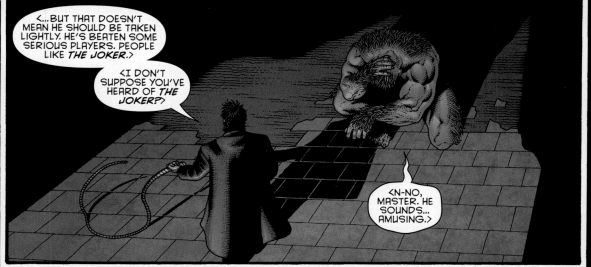

<...BUT THAT DOESN'T MEAN HE SHOULD BE TAKEN LIGHTLY. HE'S BEATEN SOME SERIOUS PLAYERS. PEOPLE LIKE *THE JOKER*.>

<I DON'T SUPPOSE YOU'VE HEARD OF *THE JOKER*?>

<N-NO, MASTER. HE SOUNDS... AMUSING.>

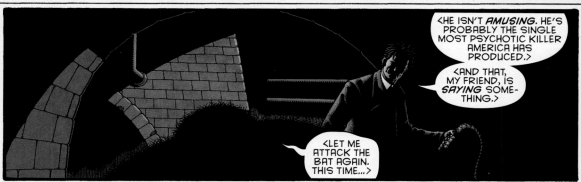

<HE ISN'T *AMUSING.* HE'S PROBABLY THE SINGLE MOST PSYCHOTIC KILLER AMERICA HAS PRODUCED.>

<AND THAT, MY FRIEND, IS *SAYING* SOMETHING.>

<LET ME ATTACK THE BAT AGAIN. THIS TIME...>

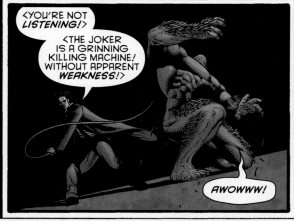

<YOU'RE NOT *LISTENING!*>

<THE JOKER IS A GRINNING KILLING MACHINE! WITHOUT APPARENT *WEAKNESS!*>

AWOWWW!

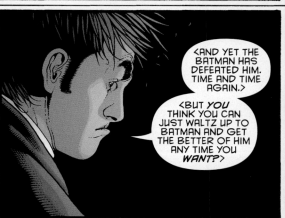

<AND YET THE BATMAN HAS DEFEATED HIM. TIME AND TIME AGAIN.>

<BUT *YOU* THINK YOU CAN JUST WALTZ UP TO BATMAN AND GET THE BETTER OF HIM ANY TIME YOU *WANT?*>

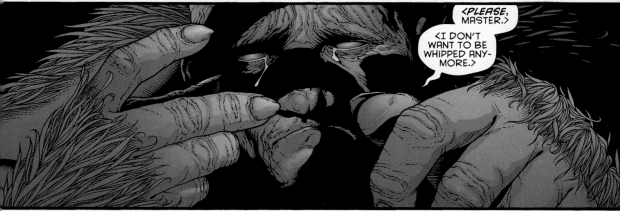

<PLEASE, MASTER.>

<I DON'T WANT TO BE WHIPPED ANY-MORE.>

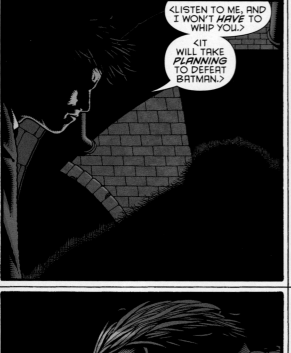

‹LISTEN TO ME, AND I WON'T *HAVE* TO WHIP YOU.›

‹IT WILL TAKE *PLANNING* TO DEFEAT BATMAN.›

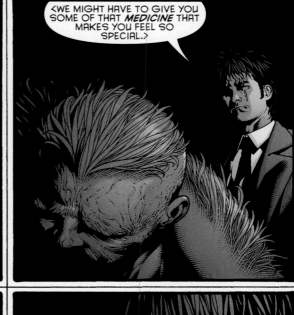

‹WE MIGHT HAVE TO GIVE YOU SOME OF THAT *MEDICINE* THAT MAKES YOU FEEL SO SPECIAL.›

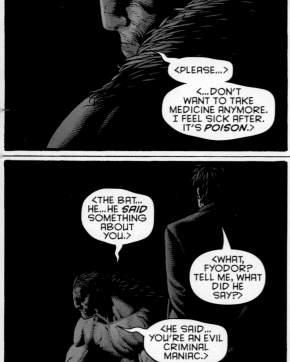

‹PLEASE...›

‹...DON'T WANT TO TAKE MEDICINE ANYMORE. I FEEL SICK AFTER. IT'S *POISON*.›

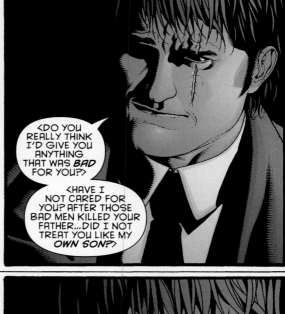

‹DO YOU REALLY THINK I'D GIVE YOU ANYTHING THAT WAS *BAD* FOR YOU?›

‹HAVE I NOT CARED FOR YOU? AFTER THOSE BAD MEN KILLED YOUR FATHER...DID I NOT TREAT YOU LIKE MY *OWN SON*?›

‹THE BAT... HE...HE *SAID* SOMETHING ABOUT YOU.›

‹WHAT, FYODOR? TELL ME, WHAT DID HE SAY?›

‹HE SAID... YOU'RE AN EVIL CRIMINAL MANIAC.›

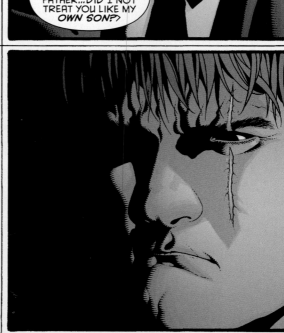

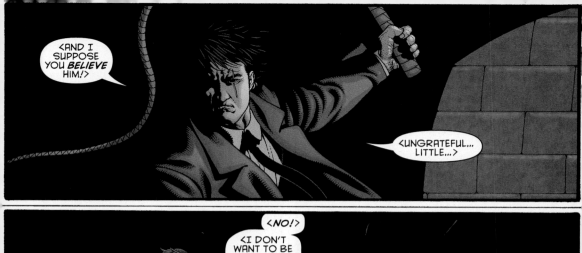

‹AND I SUPPOSE YOU *BELIEVE* HIM!›

‹UNGRATEFUL... LITTLE...›

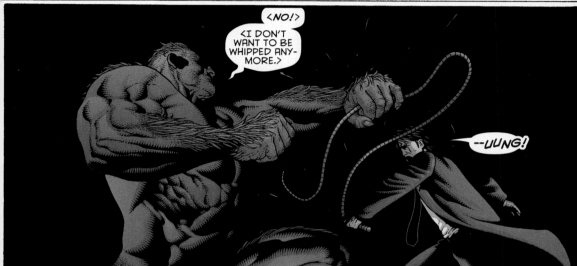

‹*NO!*›

‹I DON'T WANT TO BE WHIPPED ANY-MORE.›

*--UUNG!*

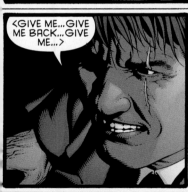

‹GIVE ME...GIVE ME BACK...GIVE ME...›

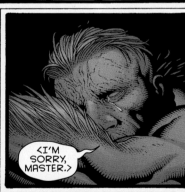

‹I'M SORRY, MASTER.›

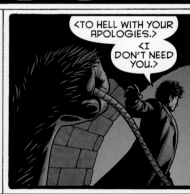

‹TO HELL WITH YOUR APOLOGIES.›

‹I DON'T NEED YOU.›

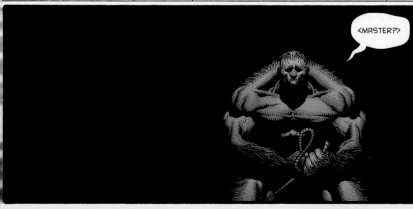

‹MASTER?›

GH... GGG... GGG
--ARRGGHH!
GGG! GGG... GGG...!
... GNNN!... HKKK!
<... THIRTY ONE, THIRTY TWO...>
<... THIRTY THREE...>

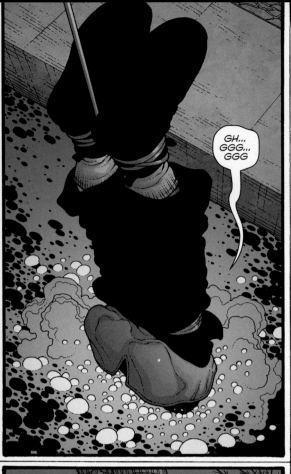

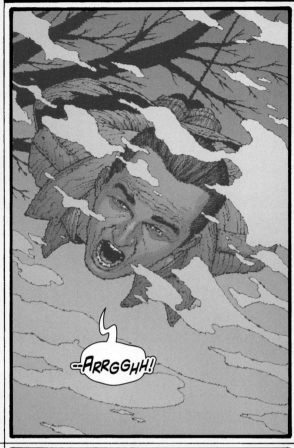

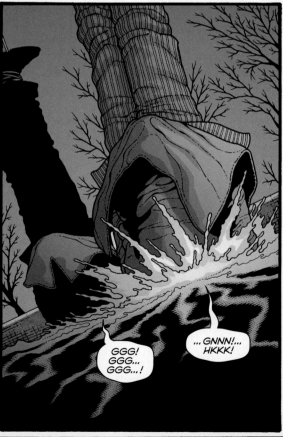

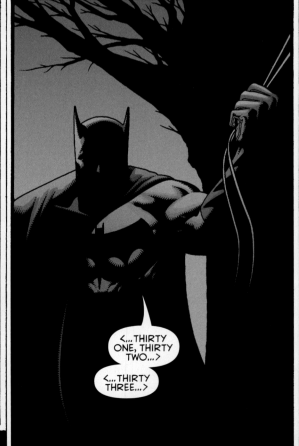

AHHH!
AGHH! HAGUHH!
<AKK... OH...OH, MERCY...>
<P-PLEASE! ANY-GHKK!-THING, W-WE'LL GIVE YOU... ANYTHING...>
<GOOD. THAT'S GOOD.>
<YOU KNOW WHAT I WANT.>
<A-ANYTHING BUT THAT.>
<DON'T YOU FEAR ME YET?>
<DON'T YOU UNDERSTAND?>
<TELL THE OTHER KINGPINS I WILL BE RELENTLESS IN THE PURSUIT OF MY GOAL.>
<TELL THEM I WANT THE TSAR.>

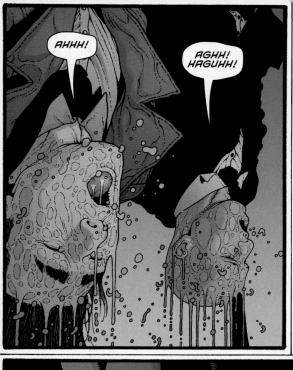

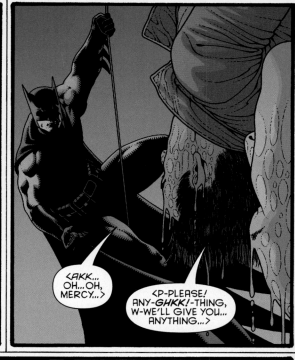

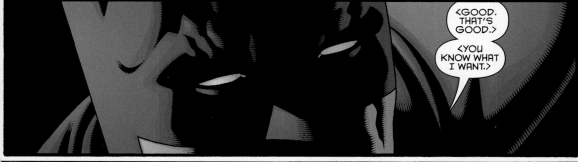

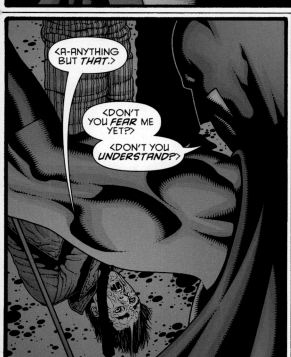

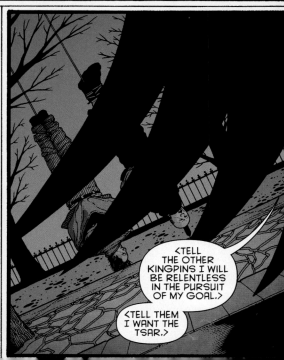

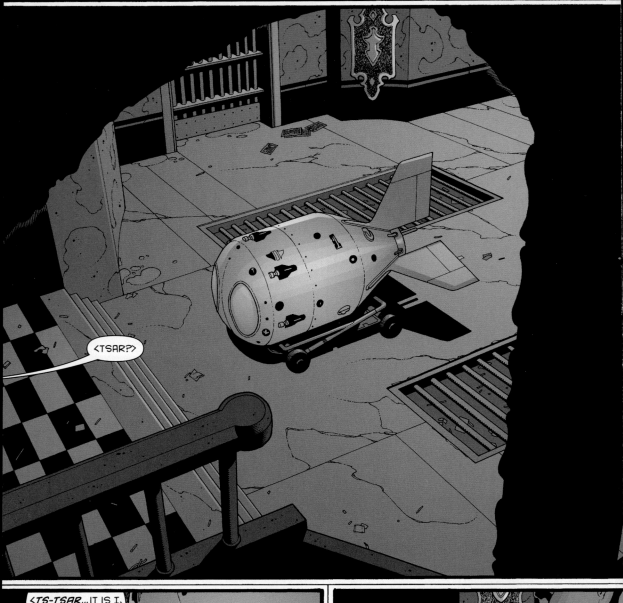

<TSAR?>

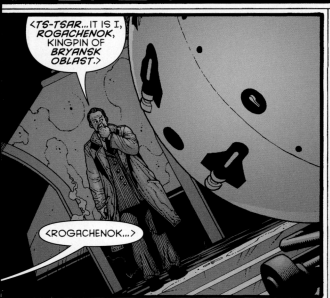

<TS-TSAR...IT IS I, ROGACHENOK, KINGPIN OF BRYANSK OBLAST.>

<ROGACHENOK...>

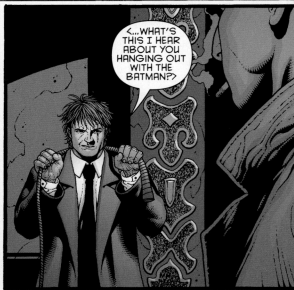

<...WHAT'S THIS I HEAR ABOUT YOU HANGING OUT WITH THE BATMAN?>

<TH-THAT'S WHY I WANTED TO SEE YOU. THE BATMAN, HE... HE'S HURTING US. EARNINGS ARE DOWN. THE KINGPINS...>
<THEY'RE... SCARED.>
<KINGPIN MEREB THE BLOODTHIRSTY HAS DEVELOPED A NERVOUS TIC. KRYUKOV THE WIDOW-MAKER...>
<...HE IS NOW TOO SCARED TO LEAVE HOME AT NIGHT.>
<I-IS THAT IT? IS... IS THAT THE BOMB?>
<NO, IT'S A RUSSIAN DOLL, YOU IDIOT.>
<WHAT THE HELL DO YOU THINK IT IS?>
KNNG KNNG KNNG
<I-ISN'T IT DANGEROUS?>
<B-BANGING IT LIKE THAT?>
<RELAX, ROGANCHENOK.>
<TELL THE OTHER KINGPINS TO RELAX, TOO.>

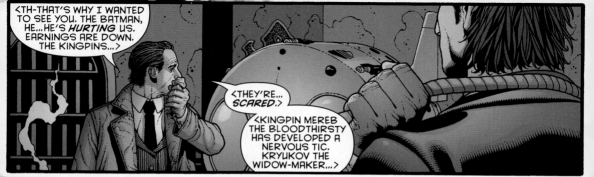

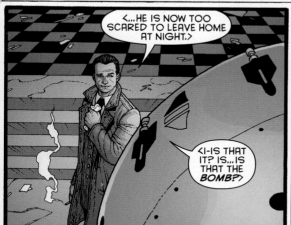

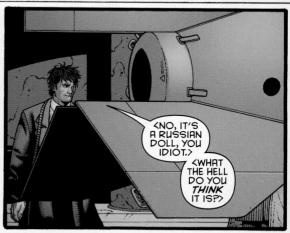

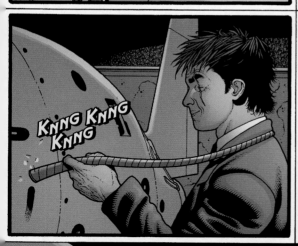

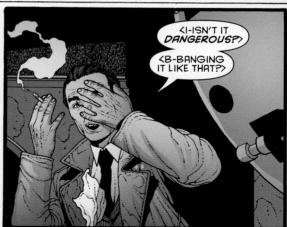

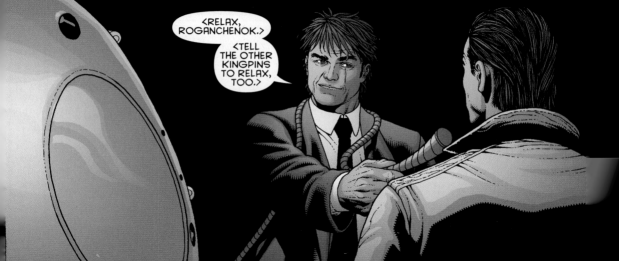

<CAN I TELL THEM THAT THE BEAR WILL KILL THE BAT?>
<SOON. RIGHT NOW THE BEAR IS GOING THROUGH A...A DIFFICULT STAGE. HOWEVER...>
<...THERE'S MORE THAN ONE PATHETIC CREATURE IN MOSCOW WHO'LL DANCE TO MY TUNE.>
Is it working?
Are they afraid of me yet?
Are they afraid enough?

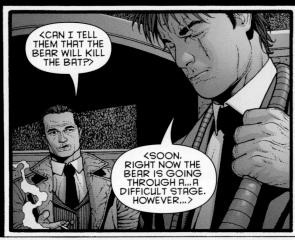

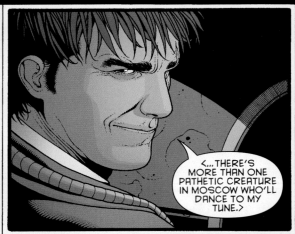

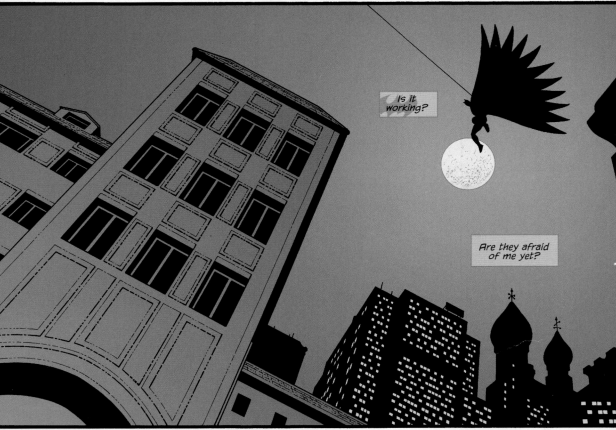

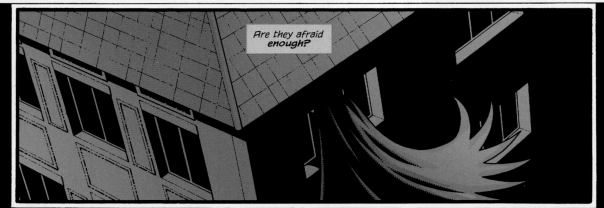

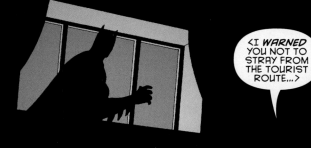

‹I *WARNED* YOU NOT TO STRAY FROM THE TOURIST ROUTE...›

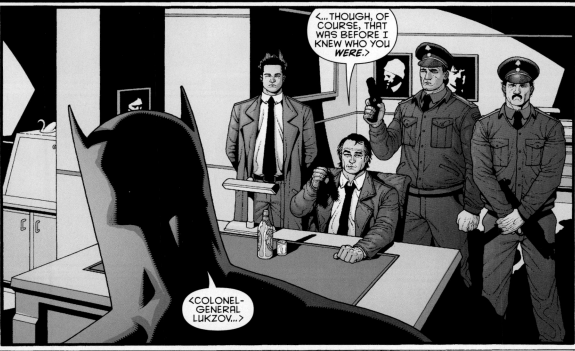

‹...THOUGH, OF COURSE, THAT WAS BEFORE I KNEW WHO YOU *WERE*.›

‹COLONEL-GENERAL LUKZOV...›

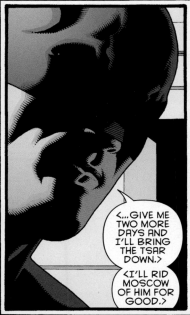

‹...GIVE ME TWO MORE DAYS AND I'LL BRING THE TSAR DOWN.›

‹I'LL RID MOSCOW OF HIM FOR GOOD.›

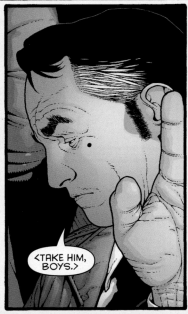

‹TAKE HIM, BOYS.›

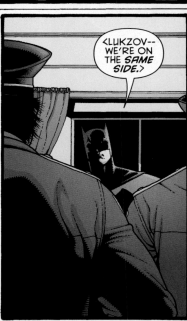

‹LUKZOV-- WE'RE ON THE *SAME* SIDE.›

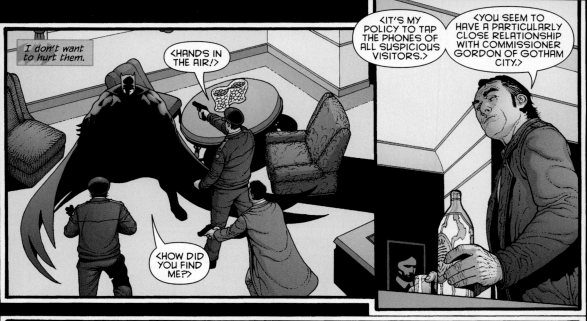

I don't want to hurt them.

<HANDS IN THE AIR!>

<HOW DID YOU FIND ME?>

<IT'S MY POLICY TO TAP THE PHONES OF ALL SUSPICIOUS VISITORS.>

<YOU SEEM TO HAVE A PARTICULARLY CLOSE RELATIONSHIP WITH COMMISSIONER GORDON OF GOTHAM CITY.>

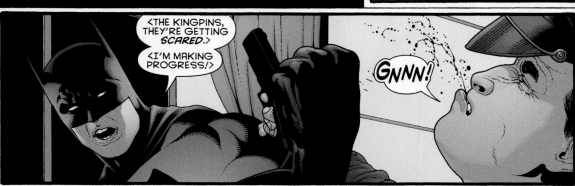

<THE KINGPINS, THEY'RE GETTING SCARED.>

<I'M MAKING PROGRESS!>

GNNN!

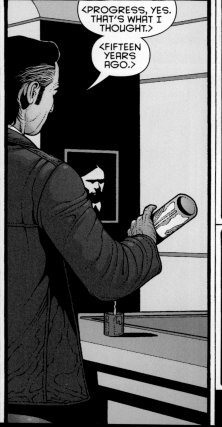

<PROGRESS, YES. THAT'S WHAT I THOUGHT.>

<FIFTEEN YEARS AGO.>

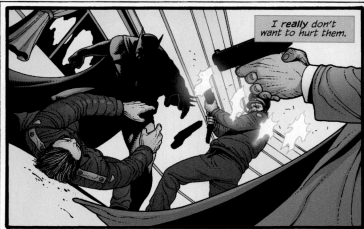

I really don't want to hurt them.

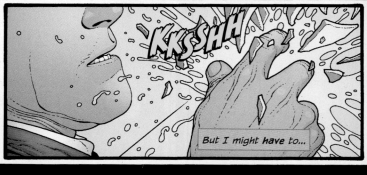

KKSSHH

But I might have to...

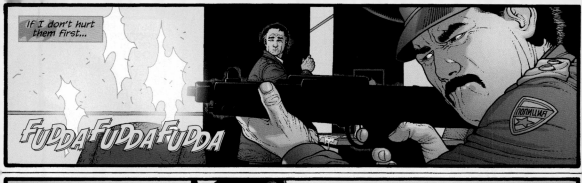

If I don't hurt them first...

FUDDAFUDDAFUDDA

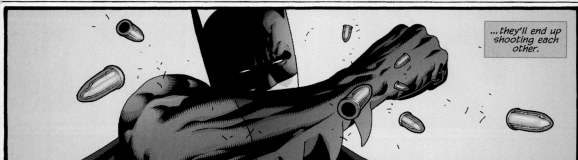

...they'll end up shooting each other.

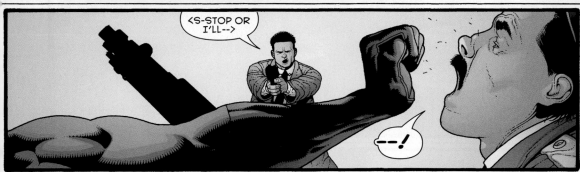

<S-STOP OR I'LL--->

--!

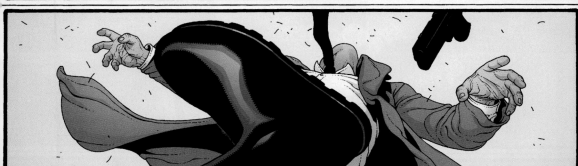

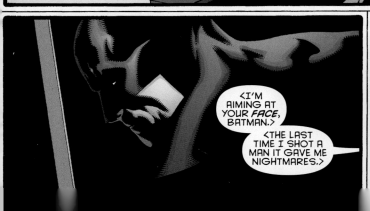

<I'M AIMING AT YOUR FACE, BATMAN.> <THE LAST TIME I SHOT A MAN IT GAVE ME NIGHTMARES.>

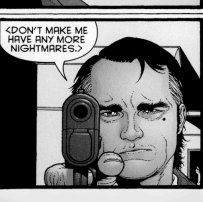

<DON'T MAKE ME HAVE ANY MORE NIGHTMARES.>

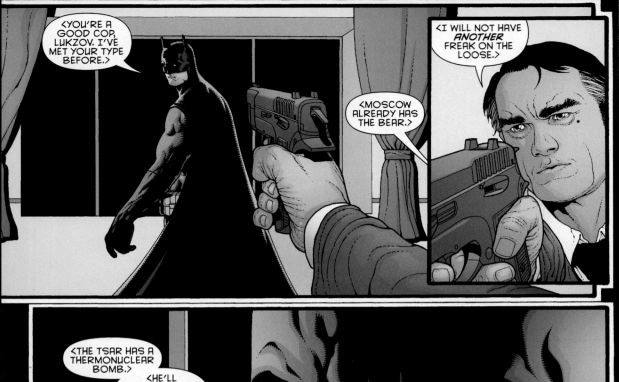

<YOU'RE A GOOD COP, LUKZOV. I'VE MET YOUR TYPE BEFORE.>

<I WILL NOT HAVE *ANOTHER* FREAK ON THE LOOSE.>

<MOSCOW ALREADY HAS THE BEAR.>

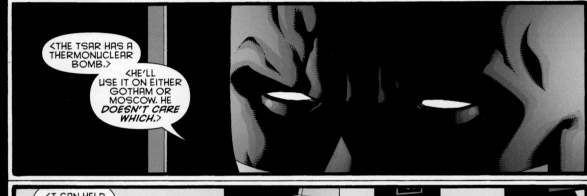

<THE TSAR HAS A THERMONUCLEAR BOMB.>

<HE'LL USE IT ON EITHER GOTHAM OR MOSCOW. HE *DOESN'T CARE WHICH.*>

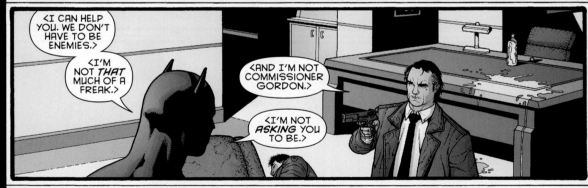

<I CAN HELP YOU. WE DON'T HAVE TO BE ENEMIES.>

<I'M NOT *THAT* MUCH OF A FREAK.>

<AND I'M NOT COMMISSIONER GORDON.>

<I'M NOT *ASKING* YOU TO BE.>

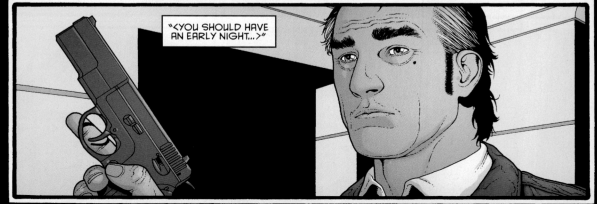

"<YOU SHOULD HAVE AN EARLY NIGHT...>"

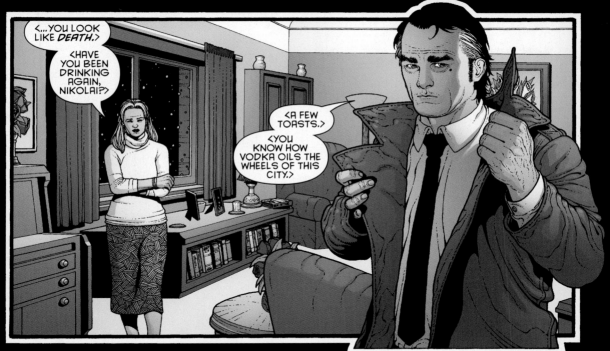

<...YOU LOOK LIKE DEATH.>

<HAVE YOU BEEN DRINKING AGAIN, NIKOLAI?>

<A FEW TOASTS.>

<YOU KNOW HOW VODKA OILS THE WHEELS OF THIS CITY.>

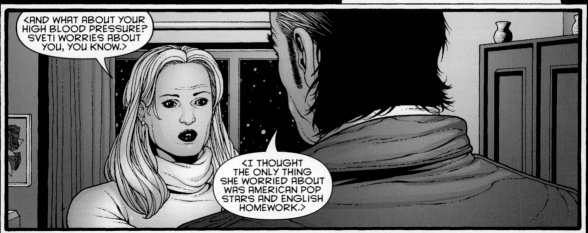

<AND WHAT ABOUT YOUR HIGH BLOOD PRESSURE? SVETI WORRIES ABOUT YOU, YOU KNOW.>

<I THOUGHT THE ONLY THING SHE WORRIED ABOUT WAS AMERICAN POP STARS AND ENGLISH HOMEWORK.>

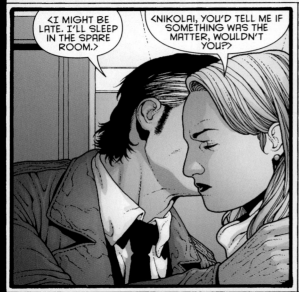

<I MIGHT BE LATE. I'LL SLEEP IN THE SPARE ROOM.>

<NIKOLAI, YOU'D TELL ME IF SOMETHING WAS THE MATTER, WOULDN'T YOU?>

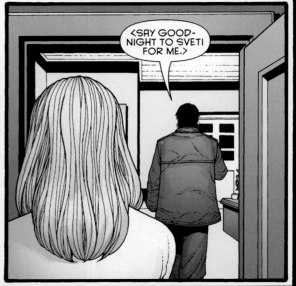

<SAY GOOD-NIGHT TO SVETI FOR ME.>

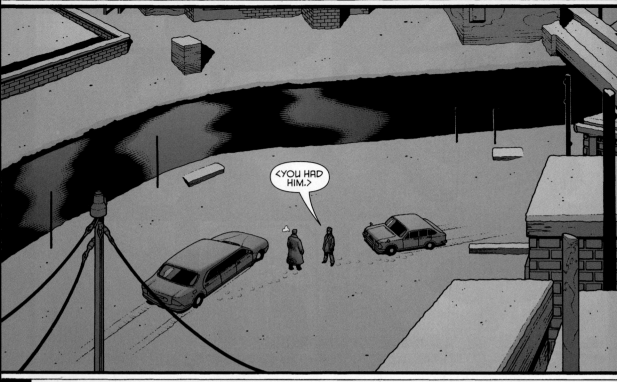

&lt;YOU HAD HIM.&gt;

&lt;YOU HAD HIM... AND YOU LET HIM GO.&gt;

&lt;HE SAID YOU HAD A *THERMONUCLEAR BOMB!*&gt;

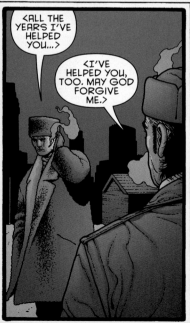

&lt;ALL THE YEARS I'VE HELPED YOU...&gt;

&lt;I'VE HELPED YOU, TOO. MAY GOD FORGIVE ME.&gt;

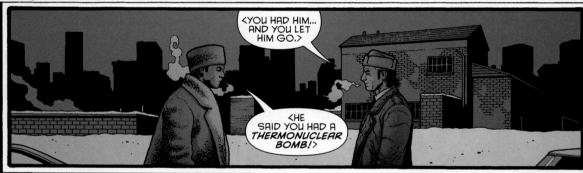

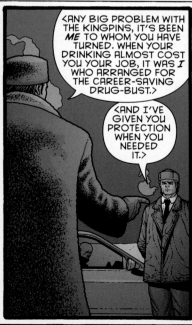

&lt;ANY BIG PROBLEM WITH THE KINGPINS, IT'S BEEN *ME* TO WHOM YOU HAVE TURNED. WHEN YOUR DRINKING ALMOST COST YOU YOUR JOB, IT WAS *I* WHO ARRANGED FOR THE CAREER-SAVING DRUG-BUST.&gt;

&lt;AND I'VE GIVEN YOU PROTECTION WHEN YOU NEEDED IT.&gt;

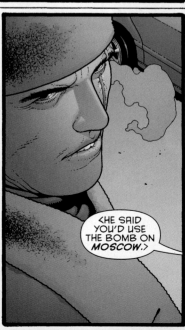

&lt;HE SAID YOU'D USE THE BOMB ON *MOSCOW.*&gt;

<ALL I WANT YOU TO DO IS ARREST HIM. AND THEN WHEN HE'S IN CUSTODY, ARRANGE FOR AN ACCIDENT TO HAPPEN.>
<WHY DON'T YOU SEND YOUR FAMOUS *BEAR* AFTER HIM?>
<I HAVE MY REASONS.>
<YOU'RE SCARED. YES, YOU'RE SCARED THAT THE BATMAN WILL BEAT HIM. THE BATMAN ISN'T SCARED OF YOU, STAVROGIN.>
<I'VE SEEN HIM UP CLOSE. I DOUBT HE'S SCARED OF *ANYTHING*.>
<I DO BELIEVE YOU'RE DEVELOPING A *THING* FOR THAT CREATURE.>
<IS *THAT* IT, COLONEL-GENERAL? IS THIS YET ANOTHER OF YOUR *WEAKNESSES?*>
<YOU *DISGUST* ME. AND I DISGUST MYSELF FOR BEING USED BY YOU. I HOPE HE *DESTROYS* YOU.>
<CAREFUL, NIKOLAI LUKZOV. THIS IS STILL MY CITY. YOU'RE STILL MY COLONEL-GENERAL.>
<GO TO HELL.>
<I BELIEVE IT IS YOU, NOT I, WHO MAY BE HEADED FOR THAT PLACE.>

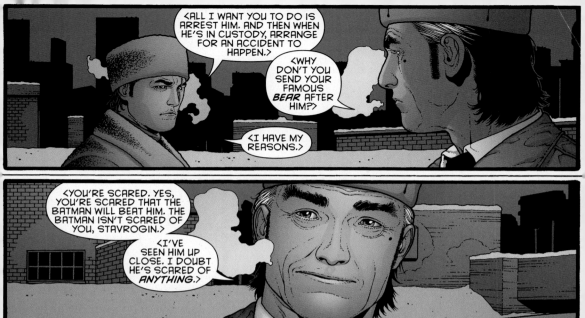

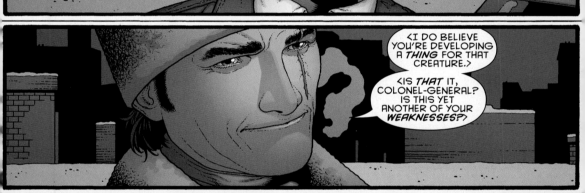

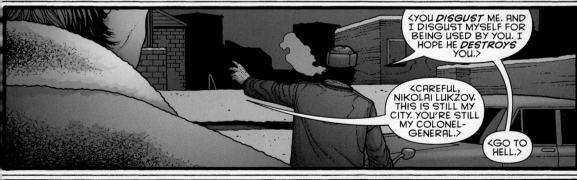

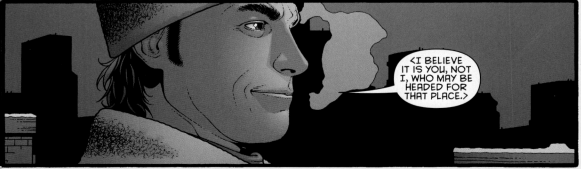

<HOW MANY YEARS HAVE I SPENT TALKING TO YOU?>
<WHAT DID I EXPECT? WHAT DID I WANT?>
<ONE OF YOU TO ANSWER BACK?>
<REMEMBER MY FATHER? H-HE WAS YOUR FATHER, TOO. HE THOUGHT HE HAD FRIENDS. THEY ALSO TURNED OUT TO BE PHANTOMS.>
<WHEN HE NEEDED THEM... WERE THEY THERE FOR HIM?>
<HELLO?>
--HHUH!
<WH-WHICH ONE OF YOU SPOKE?>
<COME ON, WHICH OF YOU PHANTOMS SPOKE?>
<NO PHANTOM, PETR.>

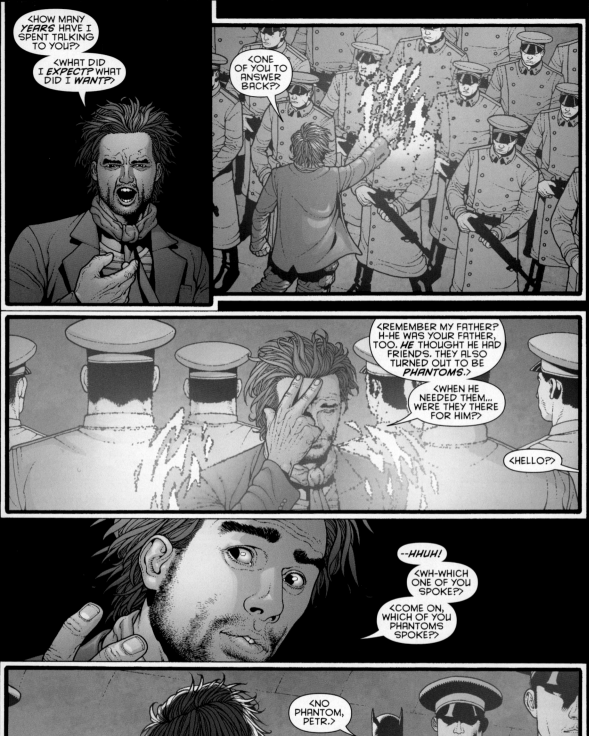

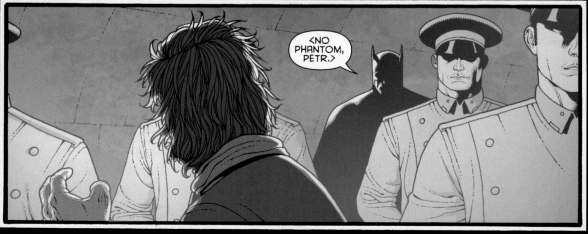

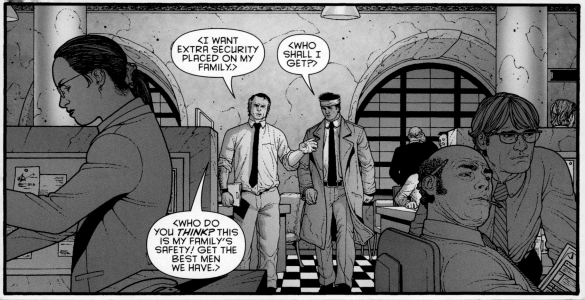

<I WANT EXTRA SECURITY PLACED ON MY FAMILY.>

<WHO SHALL I GET?>

<WHO DO YOU *THINK?* THIS IS MY FAMILY'S SAFETY! GET THE BEST MEN WE HAVE.>

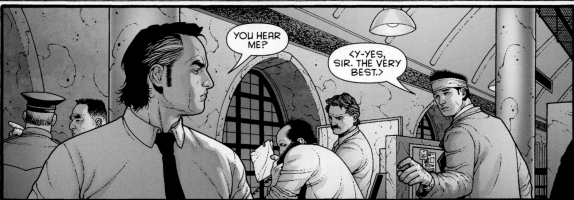

YOU HEAR ME?

<Y-YES, SIR. THE VERY BEST.>

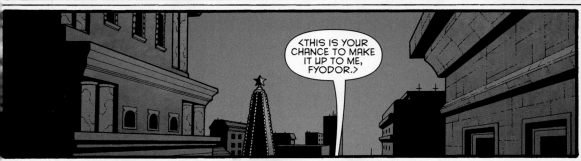

<THIS IS YOUR CHANCE TO MAKE IT UP TO ME, FYODOR.>

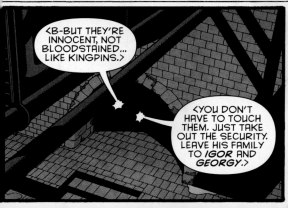

<B-BUT THEY'RE INNOCENT, NOT BLOODSTAINED... LIKE KINGPINS.>

<YOU DON'T HAVE TO TOUCH THEM. JUST TAKE OUT THE SECURITY. LEAVE HIS FAMILY TO *IGOR* AND *GEORGY*.>

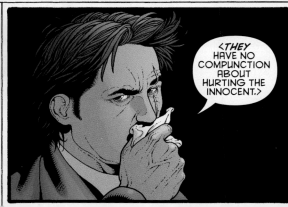

<*THEY* HAVE NO COMPUNCTION ABOUT HURTING THE INNOCENT.>

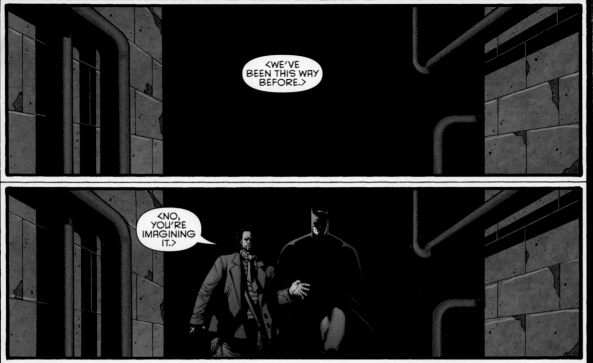

‹WE'VE BEEN THIS WAY BEFORE.›

‹NO, YOU'RE IMAGINING IT.›

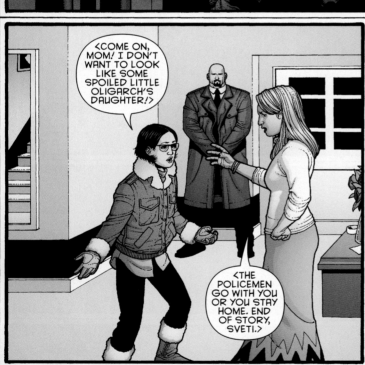

‹COME ON, MOM! I DON'T WANT TO LOOK LIKE SOME SPOILED LITTLE OLIGARCH'S DAUGHTER!›

‹THE POLICEMEN GO WITH YOU OR YOU STAY HOME. END OF STORY, SVETI.›

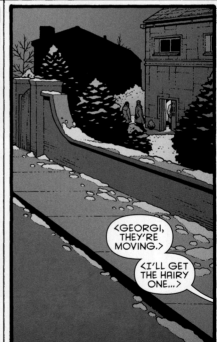

‹GEORGI, THEY'RE MOVING.›

‹I'LL GET THE HAIRY ONE...›

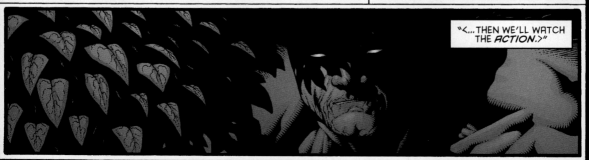

"‹...THEN WE'LL WATCH THE *ACTION*.›"

Cover by Francesco Mattina

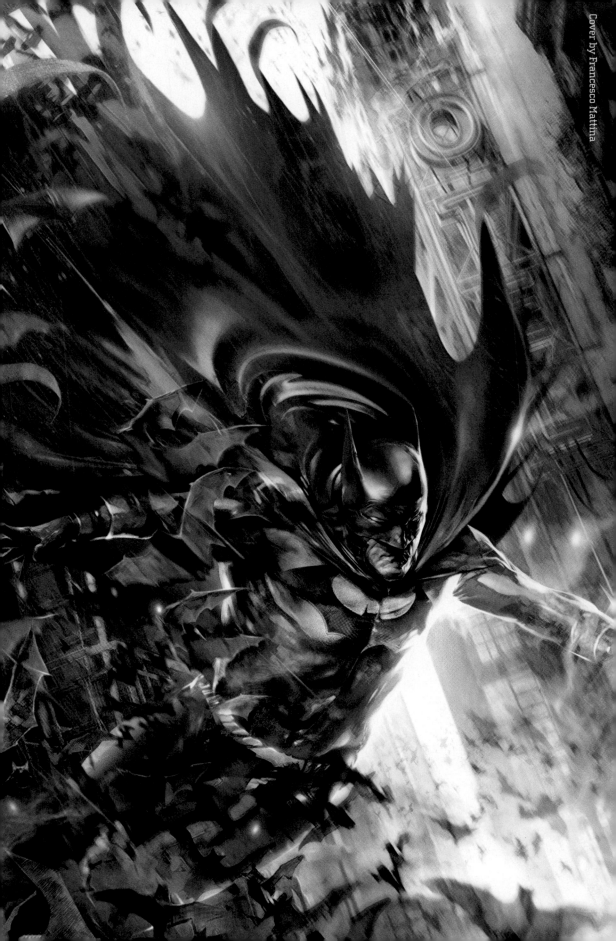

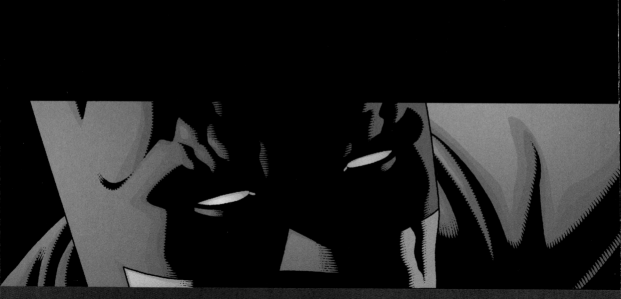

<THIS IS WHERE THE BEAR LIVES.>
<FABERGÉ.>
<YES. PITY HE DOESN'T HAVE ANYTHING VALUABLE.>
<YOU KNOW, LIKE SOME DECENT BATHROOM TISSUE. I'M RUNNING LOW ON OLD COPIES OF *PRAVDA*.>
<WHERE ELSE MIGHT HE BE?>
<IT'S A BIG PLACE AND HE'S BEEN DOWN HERE A LONG TIME. OUR BOY ONLY SHOWS HIS FACE WHEN HE HAS TO.>
<IT'S ALMOST AS THOUGH HE'S *SHY*, YOU KNOW?>
<THANKS FOR YOUR HELP, PETR.>
<YOU SHOULD STAY DOWN HERE.>
<THERE ARE A LOT OF VERY BAD MEN IN MOSCOW.>
<MY THOUGHTS EXACTLY.>
THE BAT AND THE BEAST

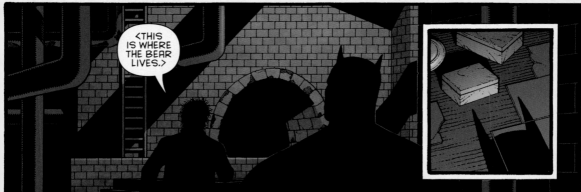

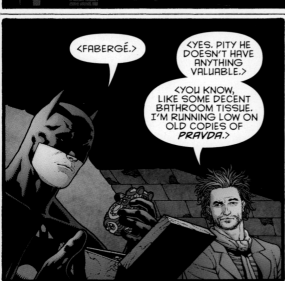

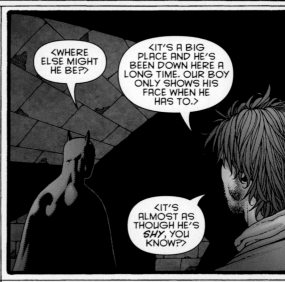

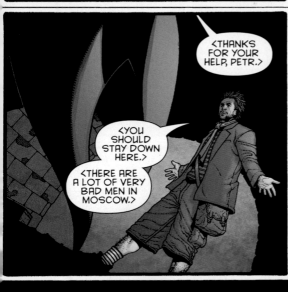

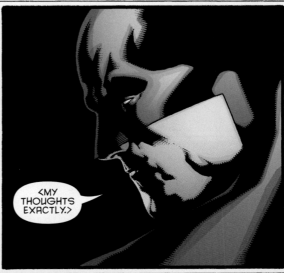

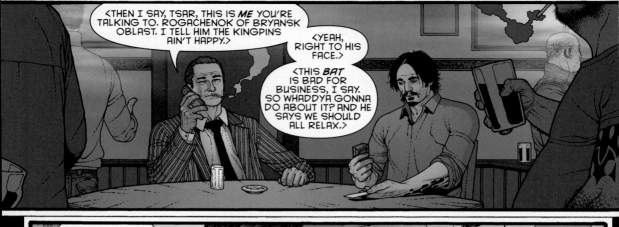

<THEN I SAY, TSAR, THIS IS *ME* YOU'RE TALKING TO. ROGACHENOK OF BRYANSK OBLAST. I TELL HIM THE KINGPINS AIN'T HAPPY.>

<YEAH, RIGHT TO HIS FACE.>

<THIS *BAT* IS BAD FOR BUSINESS, I SAY. SO WHADDYA GONNA DO ABOUT IT? AND HE SAYS WE SHOULD ALL RELAX.>

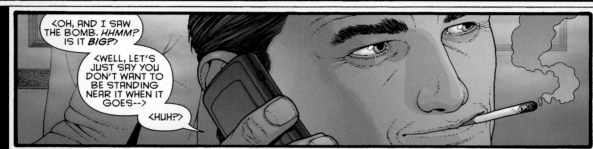

<OH, AND I SAW THE BOMB. *HHMM?* IS IT *BIG?*>

<WELL, LET'S JUST SAY YOU DON'T WANT TO BE STANDING NEAR IT WHEN IT GOES-->

<HUH?>

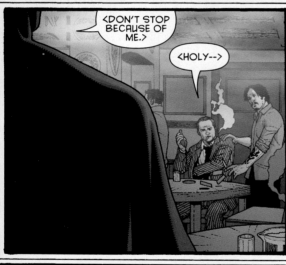

<DON'T STOP BECAUSE OF ME.>

<HOLY-->

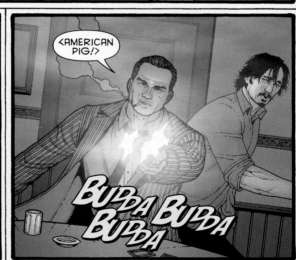

<AMERICAN PIG!>

BUDDA BUDDA BUDDA

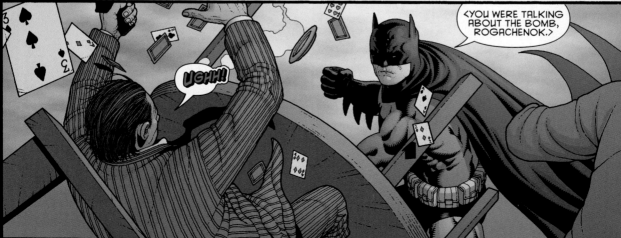

UGHH!

<YOU WERE TALKING ABOUT THE BOMB, ROGACHENOK.>

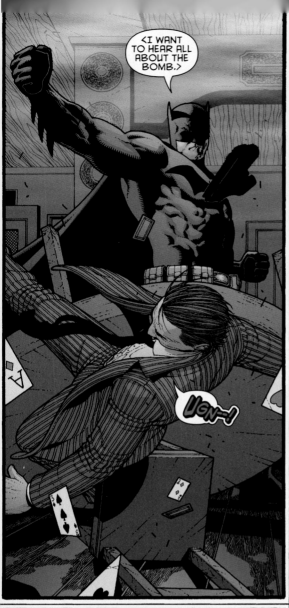

<I WANT TO HEAR ALL ABOUT THE BOMB.>

[UGN~!]

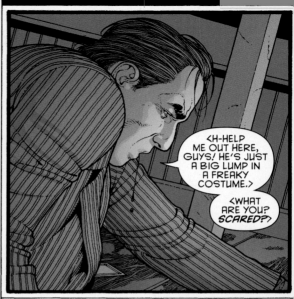

<H-HELP ME OUT HERE, GUYS! HE'S JUST A BIG LUMP IN A FREAKY COSTUME.>

<WHAT ARE YOU? SCARED?>

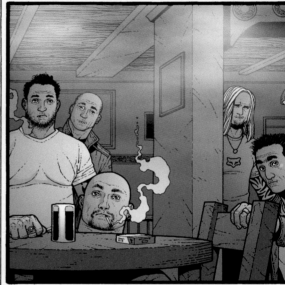

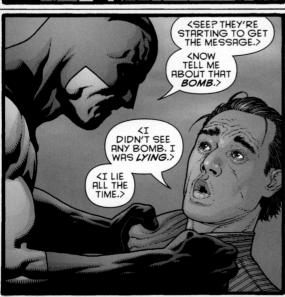

<SEE? THEY'RE STARTING TO GET THE MESSAGE.>

<NOW TELL ME ABOUT THAT BOMB.>

<I DIDN'T SEE ANY BOMB. I WAS LYING.>

<I LIE ALL THE TIME.>

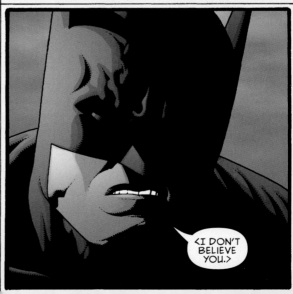

<I DON'T BELIEVE YOU.>

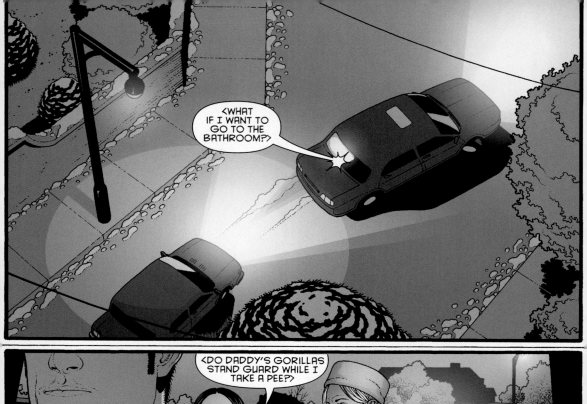

<WHAT IF I WANT TO GO TO THE BATHROOM?>

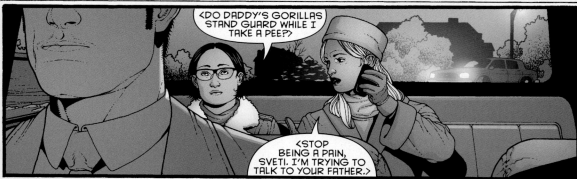

<DO DADDY'S GORILLAS STAND GUARD WHILE I TAKE A PEE?>

<STOP BEING A PAIN, SVETI. I'M TRYING TO TALK TO YOUR FATHER.>

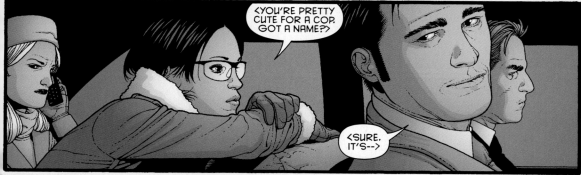

<YOU'RE PRETTY CUTE FOR A COP. GOT A NAME?>

<SURE. IT'S--->

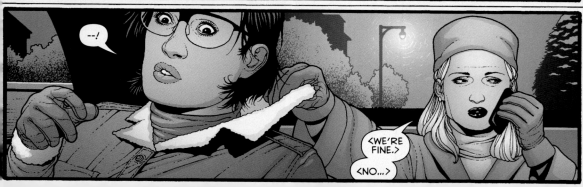

--!

<WE'RE FINE.>

<NO...>

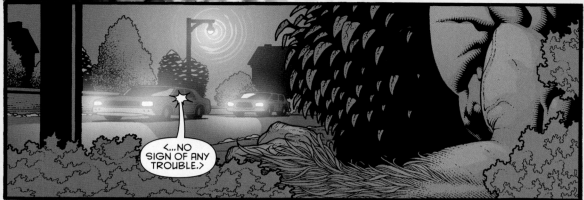

&lt;...NO SIGN OF ANY TROUBLE.&gt;

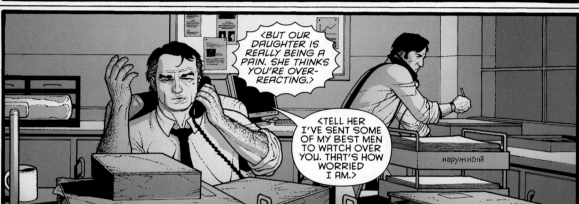

&lt;BUT OUR DAUGHTER IS REALLY BEING A PAIN. SHE THINKS YOU'RE OVER-REACTING.&gt;

&lt;TELL HER I'VE SENT SOME OF MY BEST MEN TO WATCH OVER YOU. THAT'S HOW WORRIED I AM.&gt;

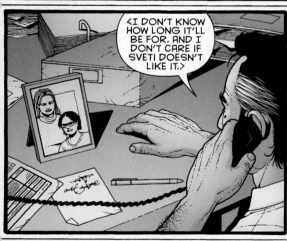

&lt;I DON'T KNOW HOW LONG IT'LL BE FOR. AND I DON'T CARE IF SVETI DOESN'T LIKE IT.&gt;

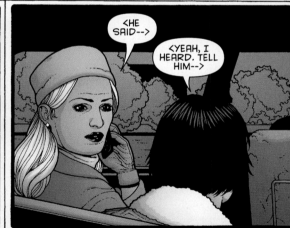

&lt;HE SAID--&gt;

&lt;YEAH, I HEARD. TELL HIM--&gt;

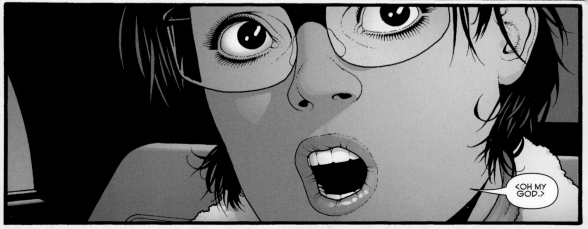

&lt;OH MY GOD.&gt;

<WHAT'S THAT? WHAT'S HAPPENING?>
"<ANNA?>"
ARRGHHH!

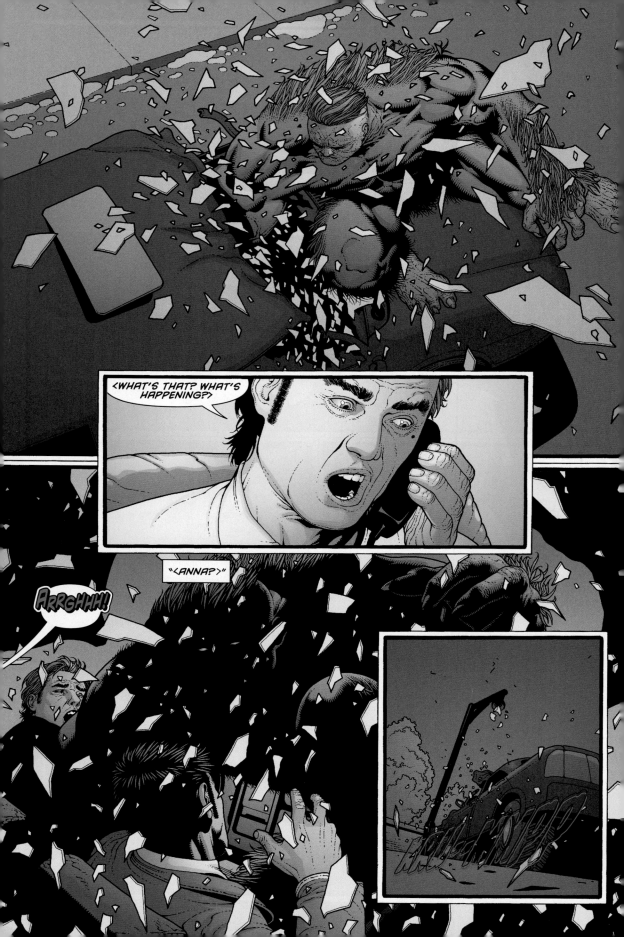

<CAR TWO, WE HAVE A *PROBLEM*.>
<WHAT'S HAPPENING THERE?>
<WHAT THE HELL IS-->
<MY GODFATHERS!>

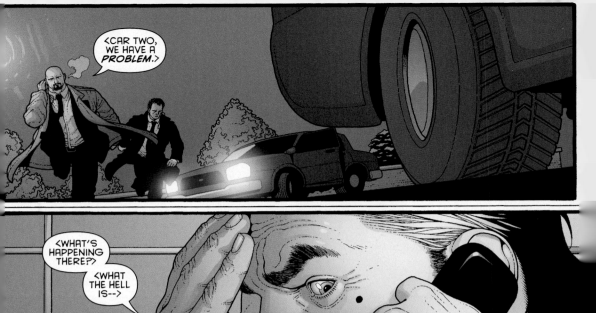

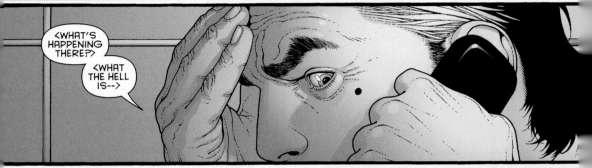

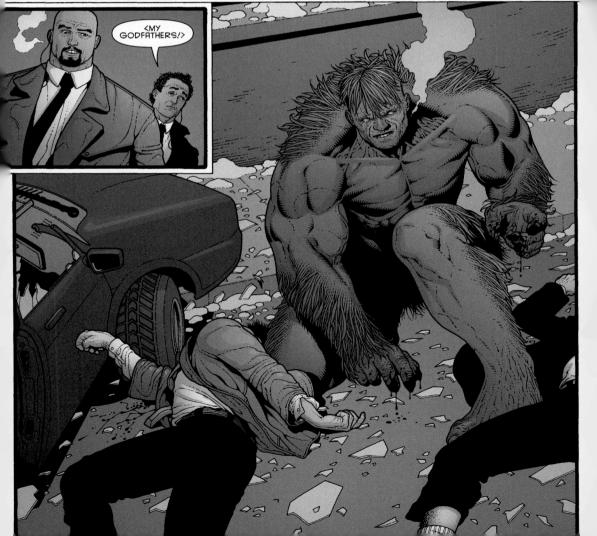

<THE TSAR KILLED HIS FATHER?>
<WHAT I HEARD, THE FATHER TREATED THAT HAIRY KID WORSE THAN ANYONE.>
<I MEAN, OKAY, HE WAS A FREAK, BUT HE WAS STILL HIS *SON*, RIGHT?>
<THE BEAR'S DAD, HE STILL THOUGHT WE WERE BACK IN THE OLD DAYS.>
<WHEN THE SOVIET UNION TRIED TO WIN THE COLD WAR WITH OLYMPIC MEDALS.>
<IS THIS IT?>
<Y-YEAH.>
<IF YOU GET THROUGH HIS SECURITY IN ONE PIECE... P-PLEASE... PLEASE DON'T TELL HIM IT WAS *ME* WHO BROUGHT YOU HERE...>
<I-I GOT A WIFE AND TWO GIRLFRIENDS WHO DEPEND ON ME.>
"<YOU DON'T KNOW WHAT THE TSAR'S LIKE.>"
<GOOD WORK. ARE BOTH OF OUR GUESTS WELL?>
<UPSET? YES, I SHOULD IMAGINE THEY'RE VERY-->
<RASIF, GO SEE WHAT ALL THAT NOISE IS ABOUT.>
BUDDA BUDDA BUDDA

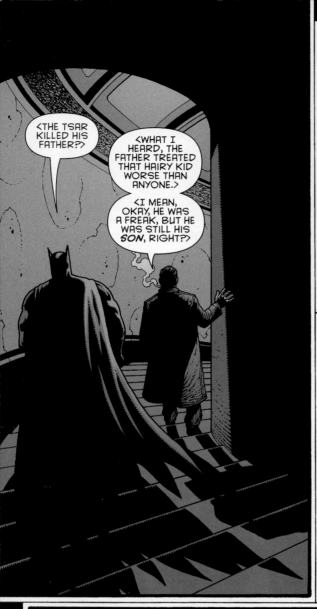

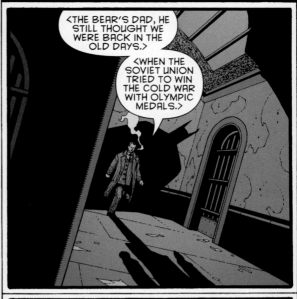

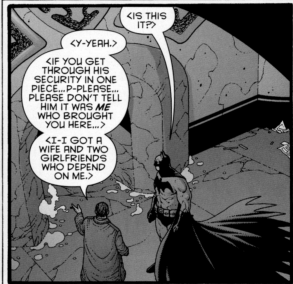

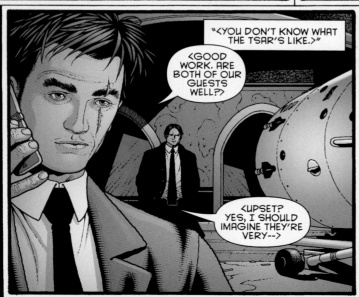

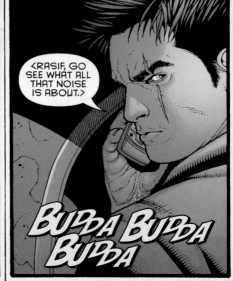

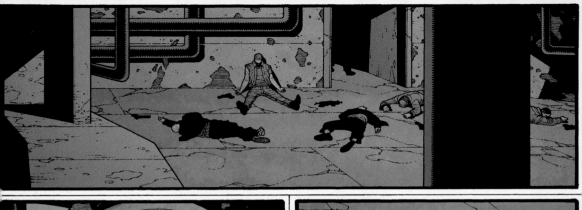

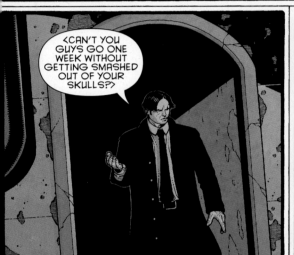

&lt;CAN'T YOU GUYS GO ONE WEEK WITHOUT GETTING SMASHED OUT OF YOUR SKULLS?&gt;

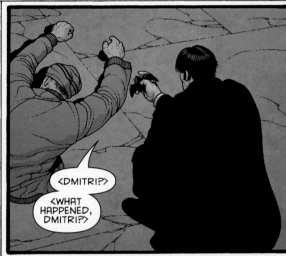

&lt;DMITRI?&gt;

&lt;WHAT HAPPENED, DMITRI?&gt;

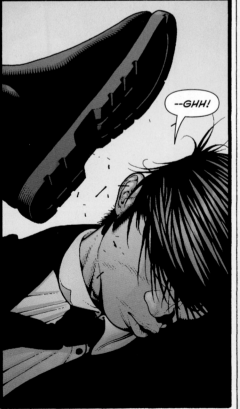

--GHH!

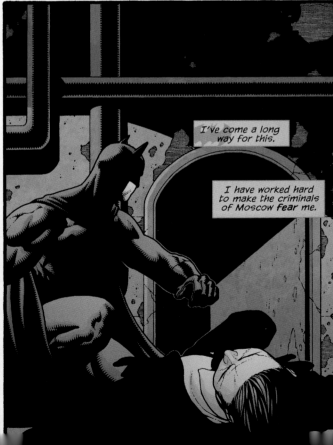

I've come a long way for this.

I have worked hard to make the criminals of Moscow *fear* me.

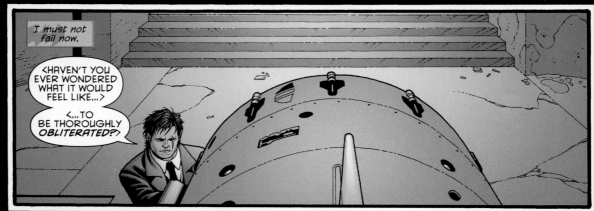

I must not fail now.

<HAVEN'T YOU EVER WONDERED WHAT IT WOULD FEEL LIKE...>

<...TO BE THOROUGHLY *OBLITERATED*?>

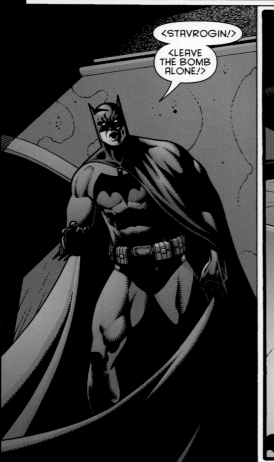

<STAVROGIN!>

<LEAVE THE BOMB ALONE!>

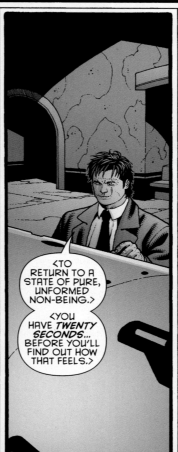

<TO RETURN TO A STATE OF PURE, UNFORMED NON-BEING.>

<YOU HAVE *TWENTY SECONDS*... BEFORE YOU'LL FIND OUT HOW THAT FEELS.>

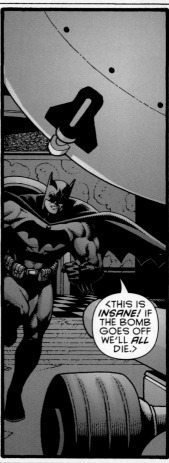

<THIS IS *INSANE!* IF THE BOMB GOES OFF WE'LL *ALL* DIE.>

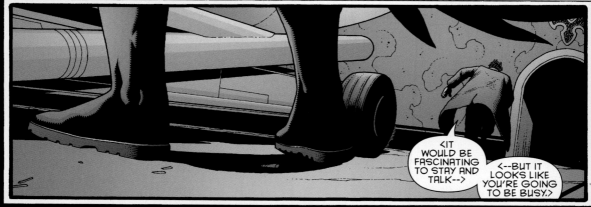

<IT WOULD BE FASCINATING TO STAY AND TALK-->

<--BUT IT LOOKS LIKE YOU'RE GOING TO BE BUSY.>

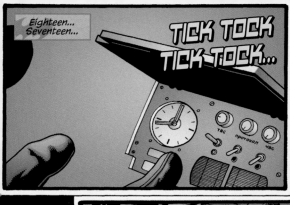

Eighteen... Seventeen...

TICK TOCK TICK TOCK...

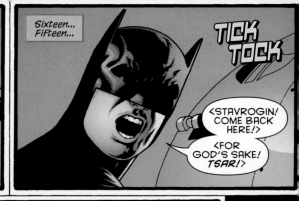

Sixteen... Fifteen...

TICK TOCK

<STAVROGIN! COME BACK HERE!>

<FOR GOD'S SAKE! TSAR!>

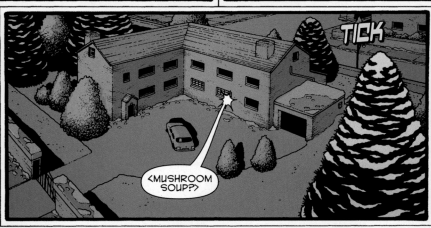

TICK

<MUSHROOM SOUP?>

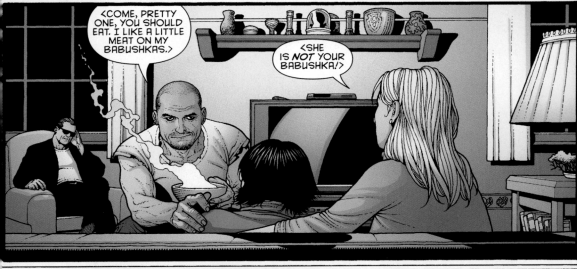

<COME, PRETTY ONE, YOU SHOULD EAT. I LIKE A LITTLE MEAT ON MY BABUSHKAS.>

<SHE IS NOT YOUR BABUSHKA!>

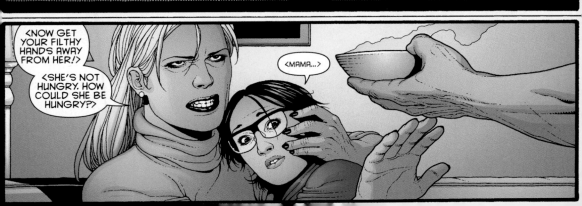

<NOW GET YOUR FILTHY HANDS AWAY FROM HER!>

<SHE'S NOT HUNGRY. HOW COULD SHE BE HUNGRY?>

<MAMA...>

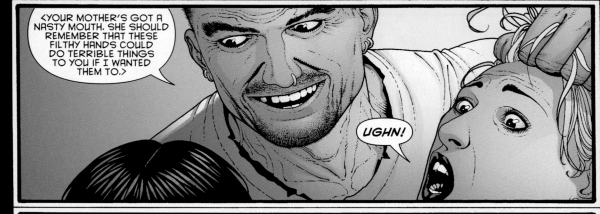

&lt;YOUR MOTHER'S GOT A NASTY MOUTH. SHE SHOULD REMEMBER THAT THESE FILTHY HANDS COULD DO TERRIBLE THINGS TO YOU IF I WANTED THEM TO.&gt;

*UGHN!*

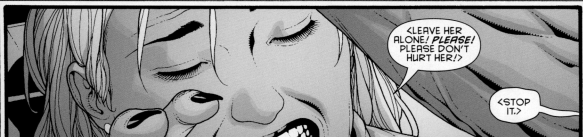

&lt;LEAVE HER ALONE! *PLEASE!* PLEASE DON'T HURT HER!&gt;

&lt;STOP IT.&gt;

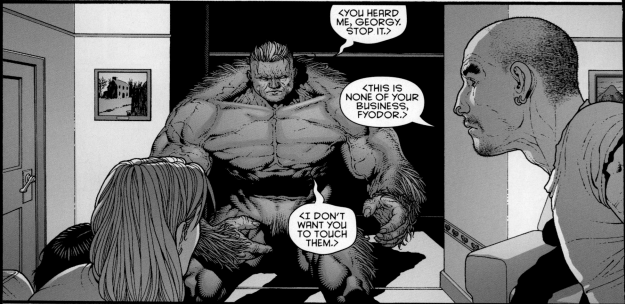

&lt;YOU HEARD ME, GEORGY. STOP IT.&gt;

&lt;THIS IS NONE OF YOUR BUSINESS, FYODOR.&gt;

&lt;I DON'T WANT YOU TO TOUCH THEM.&gt;

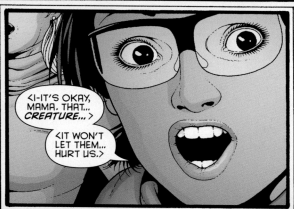

&lt;I-IT'S OKAY, MAMA. THAT... *CREATURE...*&gt;

&lt;IT WON'T LET THEM... HURT US.&gt;

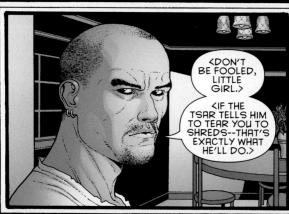

&lt;DON'T BE FOOLED, LITTLE GIRL.&gt;

&lt;IF THE TSAR TELLS HIM TO TEAR YOU TO SHREDS--THAT'S EXACTLY WHAT HE'LL DO.&gt;

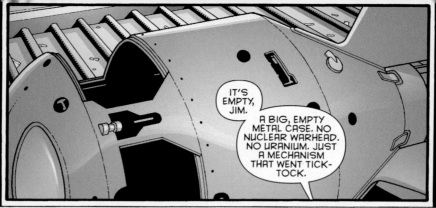

IT'S EMPTY, JIM.

A BIG, EMPTY METAL CASE. NO NUCLEAR WARHEAD. NO URANIUM. JUST A MECHANISM THAT WENT TICK-TOCK.

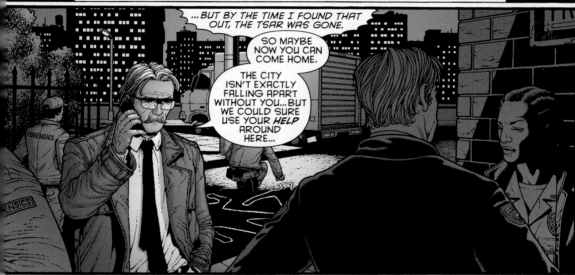

...BUT BY THE TIME I FOUND THAT OUT, THE TSAR WAS GONE.

SO MAYBE NOW YOU CAN COME HOME.

THE CITY ISN'T EXACTLY FALLING APART WITHOUT YOU...BUT WE COULD SURE USE YOUR *HELP* AROUND HERE...

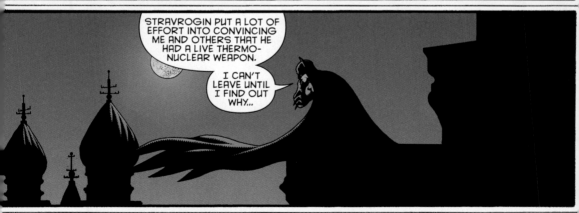

STRAVROGIN PUT A LOT OF EFFORT INTO CONVINCING ME AND OTHERS THAT HE HAD A LIVE THERMO-NUCLEAR WEAPON.

I CAN'T LEAVE UNTIL I FIND OUT WHY...

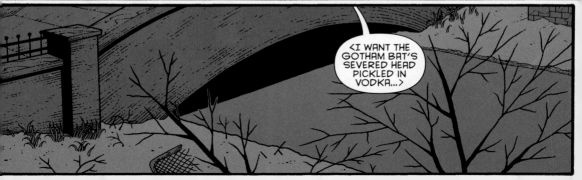

<I WANT THE GOTHAM BAT'S SEVERED HEAD PICKLED IN VODKA...>

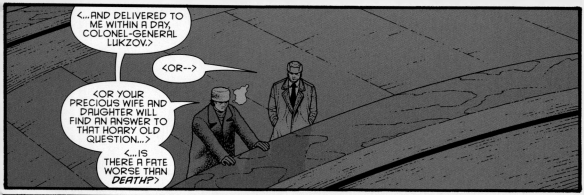

<...AND DELIVERED TO ME WITHIN A DAY, COLONEL-GENERAL LUKZOV.>

<OR--->

<OR YOUR PRECIOUS WIFE AND DAUGHTER WILL FIND AN ANSWER TO THAT HOARY OLD QUESTION...>

<...IS THERE A FATE WORSE THAN *DEATH?*>

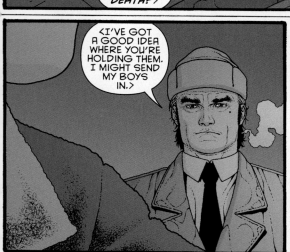

<I'VE GOT A GOOD IDEA WHERE YOU'RE HOLDING THEM. I MIGHT SEND MY BOYS IN.>

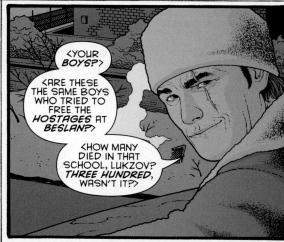

<YOUR *BOYS?*>

<ARE THESE THE SAME BOYS WHO TRIED TO FREE THE *HOSTAGES* AT *BESLAN?*>

<HOW MANY DIED IN THAT SCHOOL, LUKZOV? *THREE HUNDRED,* WASN'T IT?>

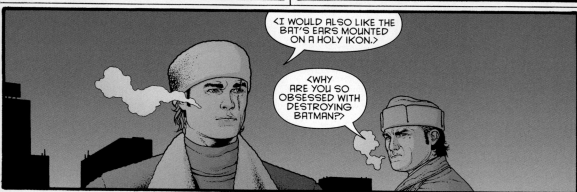

<I WOULD ALSO LIKE THE BAT'S EARS MOUNTED ON A HOLY IKON.>

<WHY ARE YOU SO OBSESSED WITH DESTROYING BATMAN?>

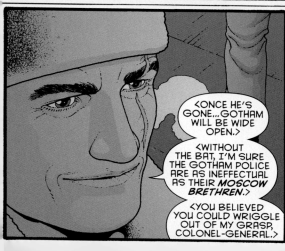

<ONCE HE'S GONE...GOTHAM WILL BE WIDE OPEN.>

<WITHOUT THE BAT, I'M SURE THE GOTHAM POLICE ARE AS INEFFECTUAL AS THEIR *MOSCOW BRETHREN.*>

<YOU BELIEVED YOU COULD WRIGGLE OUT OF MY GRASP, COLONEL-GENERAL.>

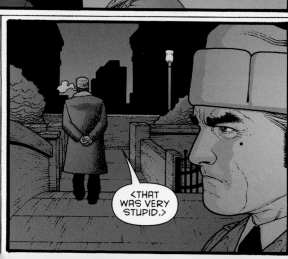

<THAT WAS VERY STUPID.>

B-BATMAN?
<I TH-THINK I KNOW HOW WE CAN BRING DOWN THE TSAR. WE NEED TO MEET AND DISCUSS.>
<I'LL BE AT THE SOUTH SIDE OF THE SOLZHENITSYN STATUE, AT THE TOP OF THE AVENUE OF DISSIDENT WRITERS. M-MEET ME THERE AT MIDNIGHT...>
<SOUNDS AS THOUGH YOU'RE SHIVERING, COLONEL-GENERAL. ARE YOU OKAY?>
<TH-THIS AVENUE IS NOTORIOUS FOR ITS *ICY WINDS*.>
<SOME SUPERSTITIOUS OLD WOMEN BELIEVE THEY ARE THE HOWLING GHOSTS OF EXECUTED WRITERS.>
<MIDNIGHT, BATMAN.>
<PLEASE DON'T LET ME DOWN.>

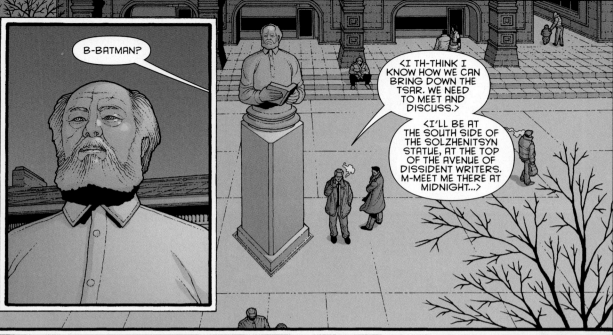

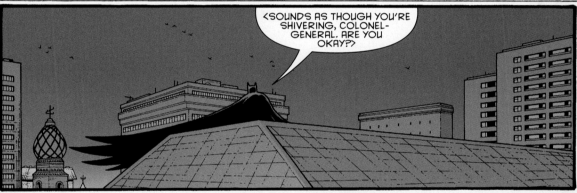

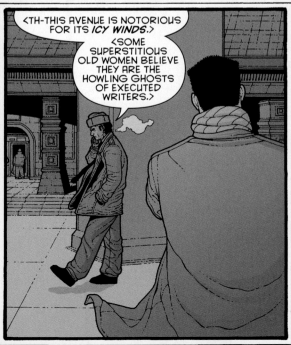

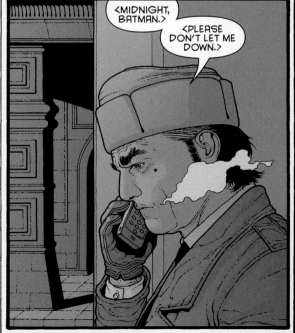

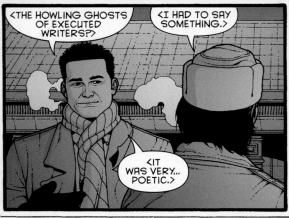

<THE HOWLING GHOSTS OF EXECUTED WRITERS?>

<I HAD TO SAY SOMETHING.>

<IT WAS VERY... POETIC.>

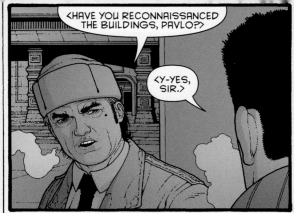

<HAVE YOU RECONNAISSANCED THE BUILDINGS, PAVLO?>

<Y-YES, SIR.>

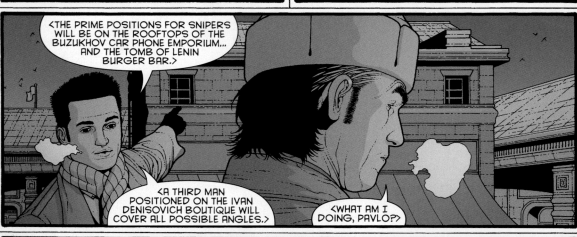

<THE PRIME POSITIONS FOR SNIPERS WILL BE ON THE ROOFTOPS OF THE BUZUKHOV CAR PHONE EMPORIUM... AND THE TOMB OF LENIN BURGER BAR.>

<A THIRD MAN POSITIONED ON THE IVAN DENISOVICH BOUTIQUE WILL COVER ALL POSSIBLE ANGLES.>

<WHAT AM I DOING, PAVLO?>

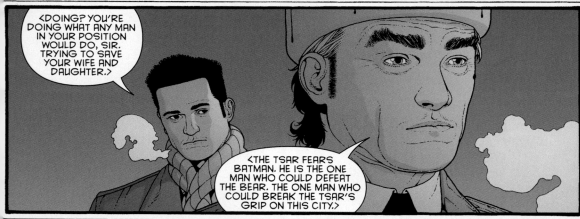

<DOING? YOU'RE DOING WHAT ANY MAN IN YOUR POSITION WOULD DO, SIR. TRYING TO SAVE YOUR WIFE AND DAUGHTER.>

<THE TSAR FEARS BATMAN. HE IS THE ONE MAN WHO COULD DEFEAT THE BEAR. THE ONE MAN WHO COULD BREAK THE TSAR'S GRIP ON THIS CITY.>

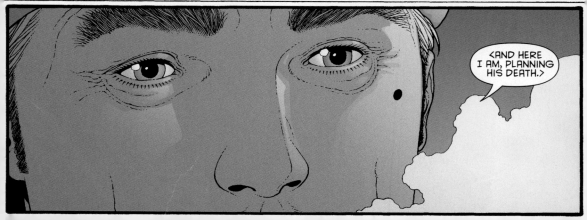

<AND HERE I AM, PLANNING HIS DEATH.>

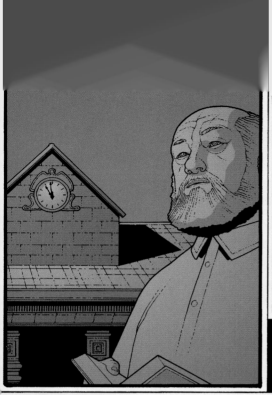

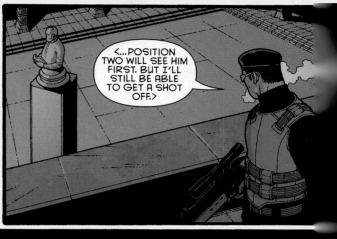

<...POSITION TWO WILL SEE HIM FIRST. BUT I'LL STILL BE ABLE TO GET A SHOT OFF.>

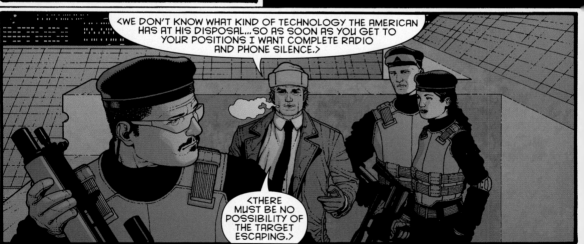

<WE DON'T KNOW WHAT KIND OF TECHNOLOGY THE AMERICAN HAS AT HIS DISPOSAL... SO AS SOON AS YOU GET TO YOUR POSITIONS I WANT COMPLETE RADIO AND PHONE SILENCE.>

<THERE MUST BE NO POSSIBILITY OF THE TARGET ESCAPING.>

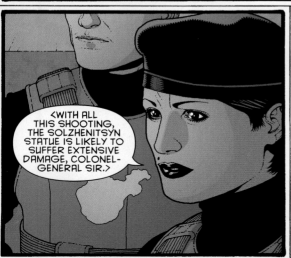

<WITH ALL THIS SHOOTING, THE SOLZHENITSYN STATUE IS LIKELY TO SUFFER EXTENSIVE DAMAGE, COLONEL-GENERAL SIR.>

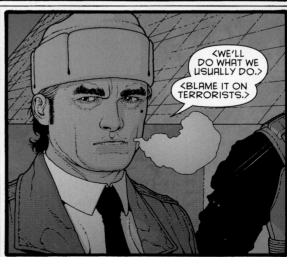

<WE'LL DO WHAT WE USUALLY DO.>

<BLAME IT ON TERRORISTS.>

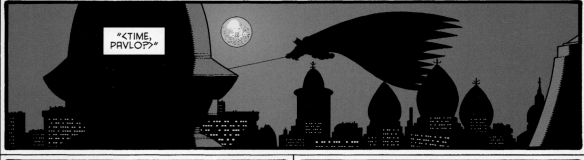

"<TIME, PAVLO?>"

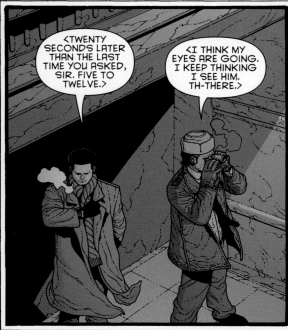

<TWENTY SECONDS LATER THAN THE LAST TIME YOU ASKED, SIR. FIVE TO TWELVE.>

<I THINK MY EYES ARE GOING. I KEEP THINKING I SEE HIM. TH-THERE.>

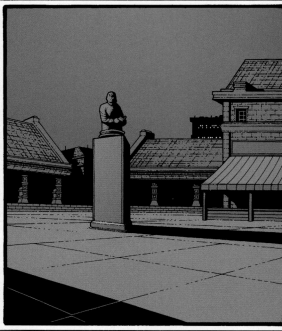

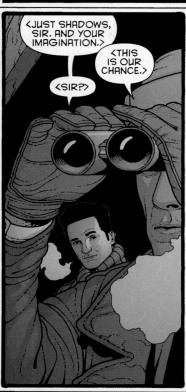

<JUST SHADOWS, SIR. AND YOUR IMAGINATION.>

<THIS IS OUR CHANCE.>

<SIR?>

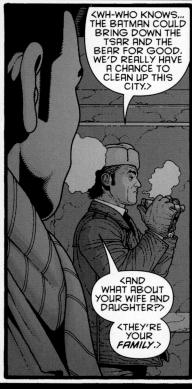

<WH-WHO KNOWS... THE BATMAN COULD BRING DOWN THE TSAR AND THE BEAR FOR GOOD. WE'D REALLY HAVE A CHANCE TO CLEAN UP THIS CITY.>

<AND WHAT ABOUT YOUR WIFE AND DAUGHTER?>

<THEY'RE YOUR FAMILY.>

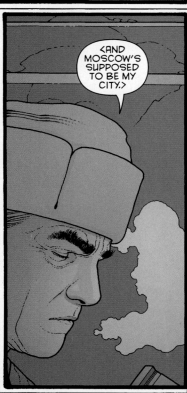

<AND MOSCOW'S SUPPOSED TO BE MY CITY.>

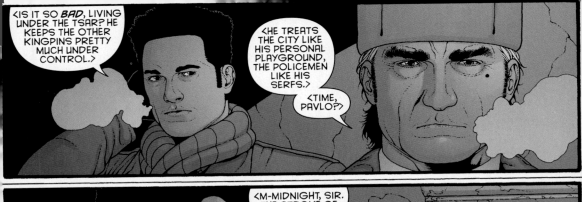

<IS IT SO *BAD*, LIVING UNDER THE TSAR? HE KEEPS THE OTHER KINGPINS PRETTY MUCH UNDER CONTROL.>

<HE TREATS THE CITY LIKE HIS PERSONAL PLAYGROUND, THE POLICEMEN LIKE HIS SERFS.>

<TIME, PAVLO?>

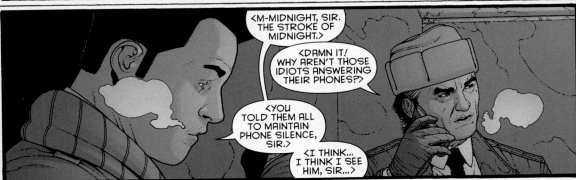

<M-MIDNIGHT, SIR. THE STROKE OF MIDNIGHT.>

<DAMN IT! WHY AREN'T THOSE IDIOTS ANSWERING THEIR PHONES?>

<YOU TOLD THEM ALL TO MAINTAIN PHONE SILENCE, SIR.>

<I THINK... I THINK I SEE HIM, SIR....>

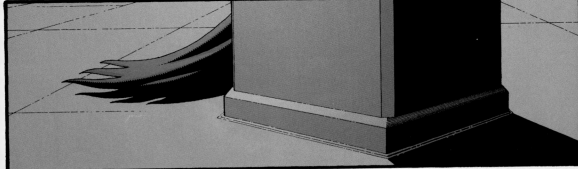

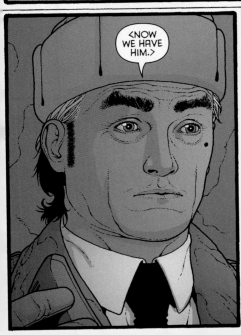

<NOW WE HAVE HIM.>

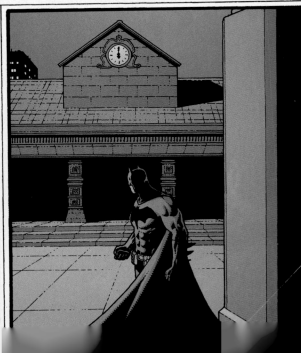

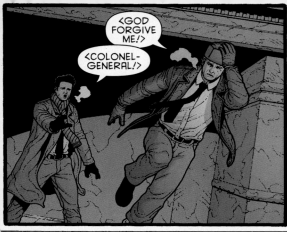

<GOD FORGIVE ME!>

<COLONEL-GENERAL!>

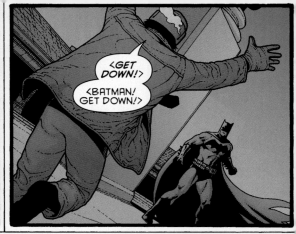

<GET DOWN!>

<BATMAN! GET DOWN!>

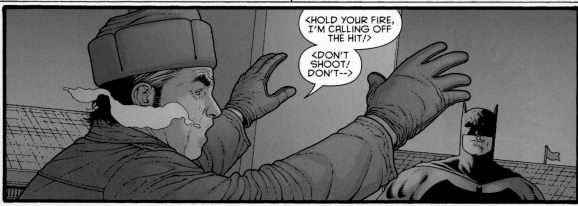

<HOLD YOUR FIRE, I'M CALLING OFF THE HIT!>

<DON'T SHOOT! DON'T-->

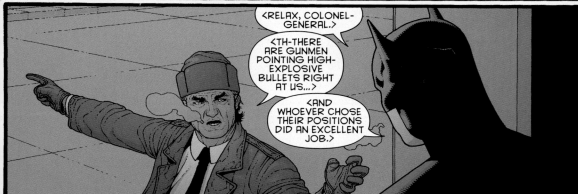

<RELAX, COLONEL-GENERAL.>

<TH-THERE ARE GUNMEN POINTING HIGH-EXPLOSIVE BULLETS RIGHT AT US...>

<AND WHOEVER CHOSE THEIR POSITIONS DID AN EXCELLENT JOB.>

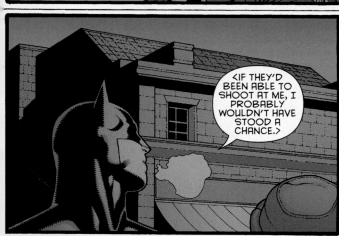

<IF THEY'D BEEN ABLE TO SHOOT AT ME, I PROBABLY WOULDN'T HAVE STOOD A CHANCE.>

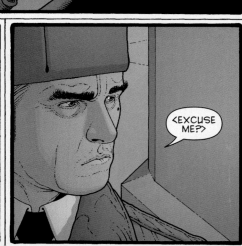

<EXCUSE ME?>

HGMMM!

<...QUITE OBVIOUS FROM YOUR VOICE THAT SOMETHING WAS WRONG. I TOOK A *PRECAUTION*...>

<...CHECKED OUT THE POSITIONS *I'D* TAKE IF I WAS TO SET A TRAP. YOU'LL FIND THE OTHER SNIPERS IN A SIMILAR CONDITION.>

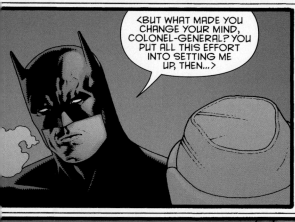

<BUT WHAT MADE YOU CHANGE YOUR MIND, COLONEL-GENERAL? YOU PUT ALL THIS EFFORT INTO SETTING ME UP, THEN...>

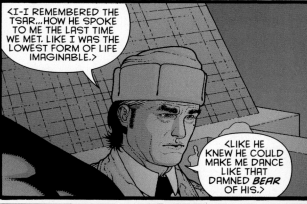

<I-I REMEMBERED THE TSAR...HOW HE SPOKE TO ME THE LAST TIME WE MET. LIKE I WAS THE LOWEST FORM OF LIFE IMAGINABLE.>

<LIKE HE KNEW HE COULD MAKE ME DANCE LIKE THAT DAMNED *BEAR* OF HIS.>

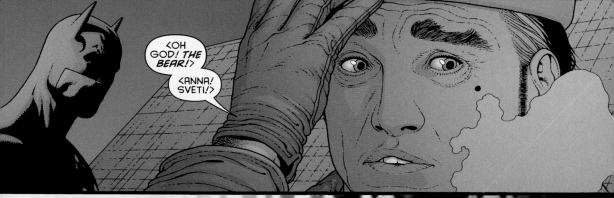

<OH GOD! *THE BEAR!*>

<ANNA! SVETI!>

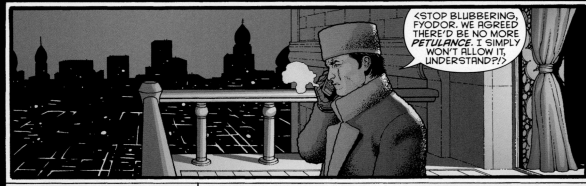

&lt;STOP BLUBBERING, FYODOR. WE AGREED THERE'D BE NO MORE *PETULANCE*. I SIMPLY WON'T ALLOW IT, UNDERSTAND?!&gt;

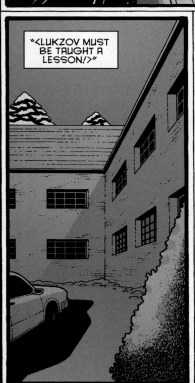

"&lt;LUKZOV MUST BE TAUGHT A LESSON!&gt;"

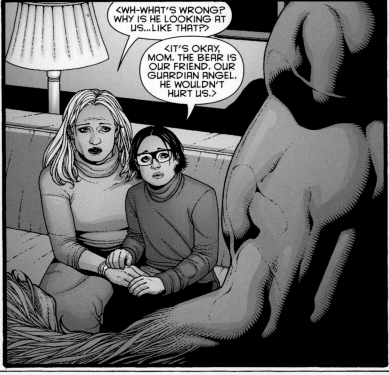

&lt;WH-WHAT'S WRONG? WHY IS HE LOOKING AT US...LIKE THAT?&gt;

&lt;IT'S OKAY, MOM. THE BEAR IS OUR FRIEND. OUR GUARDIAN ANGEL. HE WOULDN'T HURT US.&gt;

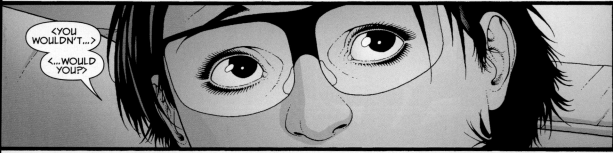

&lt;YOU WOULDN'T...&gt;

&lt;...WOULD YOU?&gt;

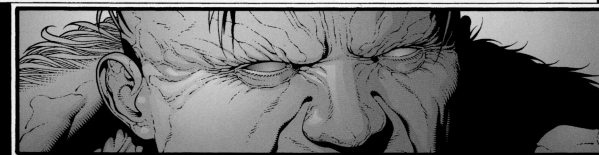

МОСКВА
ФИЗКУЛЬТУРНЫЙ ПРАЗДНИК
Cover by Francesco Mattina

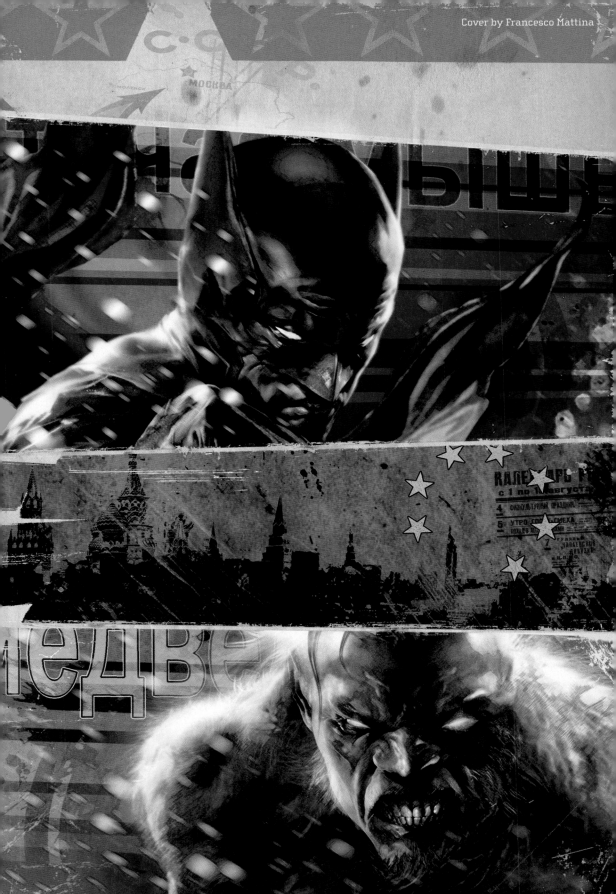

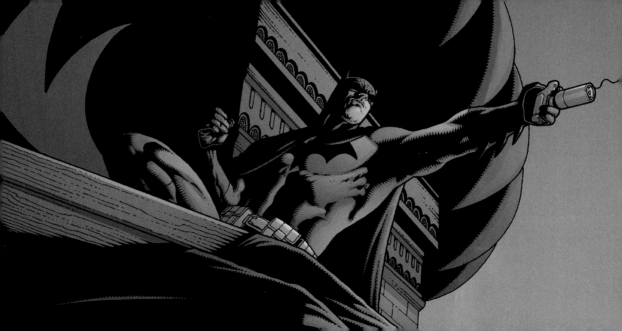

<I KNOW WHAT THE TSAR TOLD ME. I'M JUST NOT SURE IF I CAN DO IT.>
<YOU'VE TERRORIZED THE MOSCOW UNDERWORLD FOR *YEARS*. YOU RIPPED OFF KINGPIN KIRILOV'S FINGERS. YOU THREW KINGPIN ZVER OUT A FOURTH STORY WINDOW.>
<DOCTORS *STILL* CAN'T AGREE ON EXACTLY WHAT YOU DID TO KINGPIN DUBININ.>
<GEORGY'S RIGHT. TEARING THESE TWO SWEETIES LIMB FROM LIMB SHOULD PRESENT *NO* DIFFICULTIES TO A CREATURE LIKE YOU.>
<MAMA!>

# THE BAT AND THE BEAST

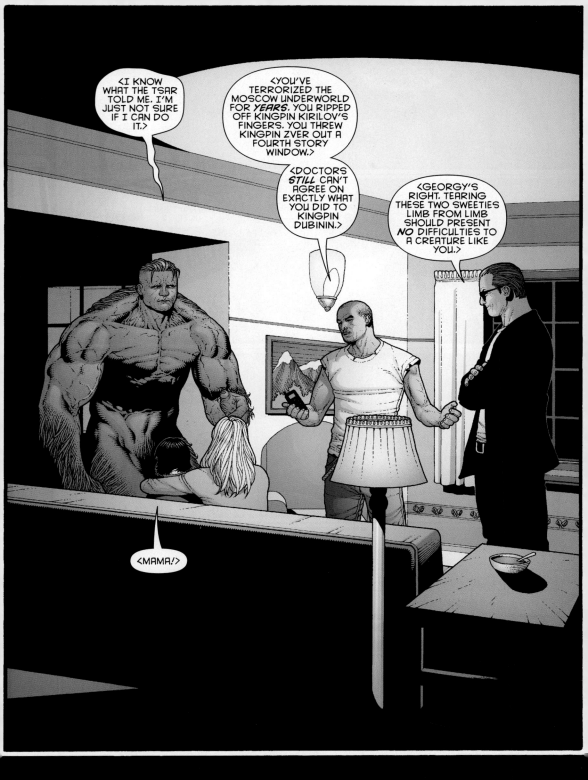

<THEY'RE DEFINITELY INSIDE, COLONEL-GENERAL. THINK I HAVE ENOUGH MEN IN POSITION TO MOVE IN-->
<LUKZOV! TELL HIM NOT TO DO ANYTHING UNTIL I GET THERE.>
<DON'T DO ANYTHING UNTIL...>
<...UNTIL *I* GET THERE!>
"<I'M SCARED, MAMA...>"
<...I'M REALLY SCARED.>
<IT'S OKAY. HE DOESN'T WANT TO HURT US. I CAN SEE IT...IN HIS *EYES*.>
<I DON'T KNOW WHY THERE'S NO BLOOD YET, SIR. HE'S HESITATING.>
<NO. WAIT. I THINK HE'S GONNA DO IT.>
<I THINK THE BEAR HAS FOUND HIS STONES...>
<CUT THE RUNNING COMMENTARY AND TELL ME HE'S TEARING THEM UP, GEORGY. TELL ME HE'S BEING *OBEDIENT*.>
<COME ON, YOU PEASANT! GIVE ME WHAT I WANT!>

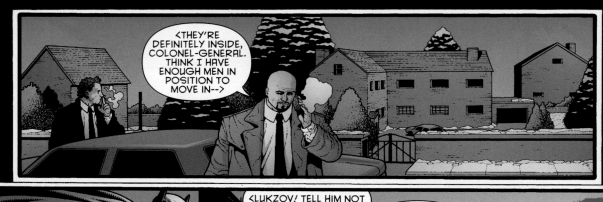

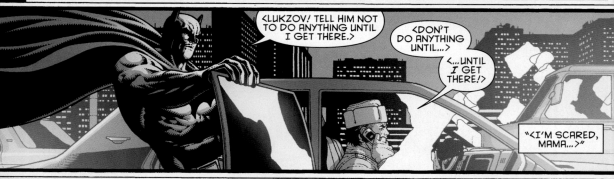

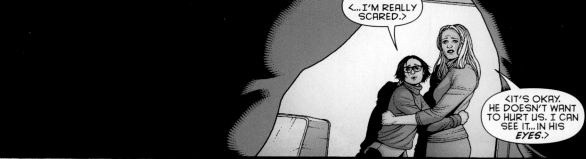

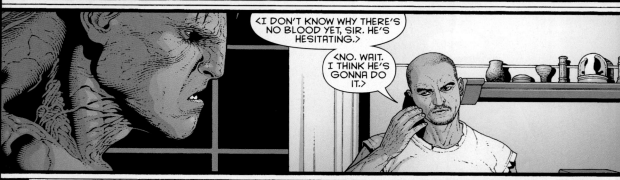

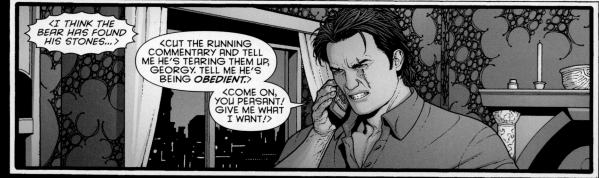

<NO NEED TO TALK TO ME LIKE THAT, SIR. IT'S NOT MY FAULT HE'S TURNING INTO A BIG BABUSHKA.>
<MOVE IT, HAIR-BALL. YOU'RE UPSETTING THE BOSS.>
AIIEE!
ARRGHH!
<SCREAMS! FOR GOD'S SAKE, THEY'VE GOT TO MOVE IN!>
<NO, HOLD BACK YOUR MEN, LUKZOV...>

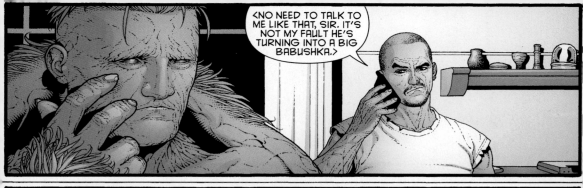

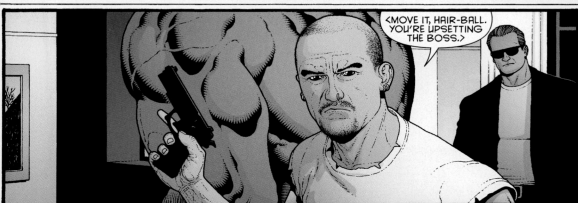

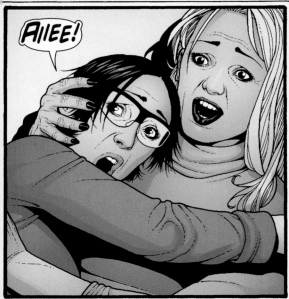

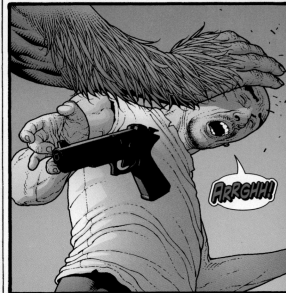

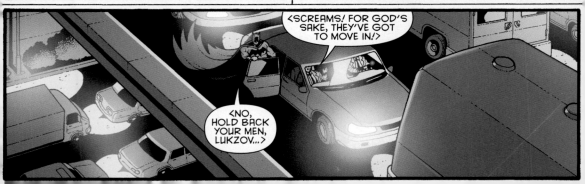

<...I'M PRETTY GOOD AT THIS STUFF.>

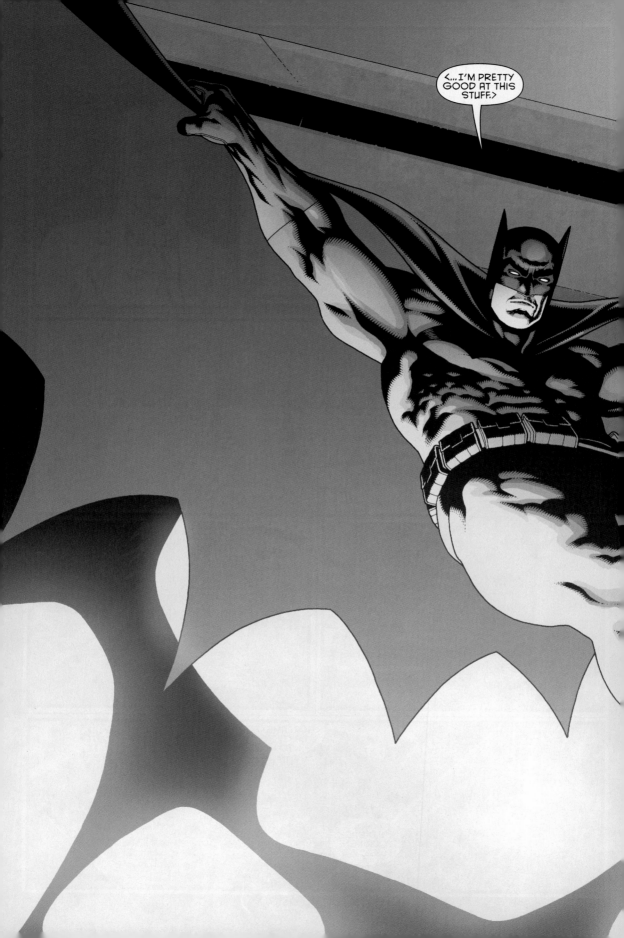

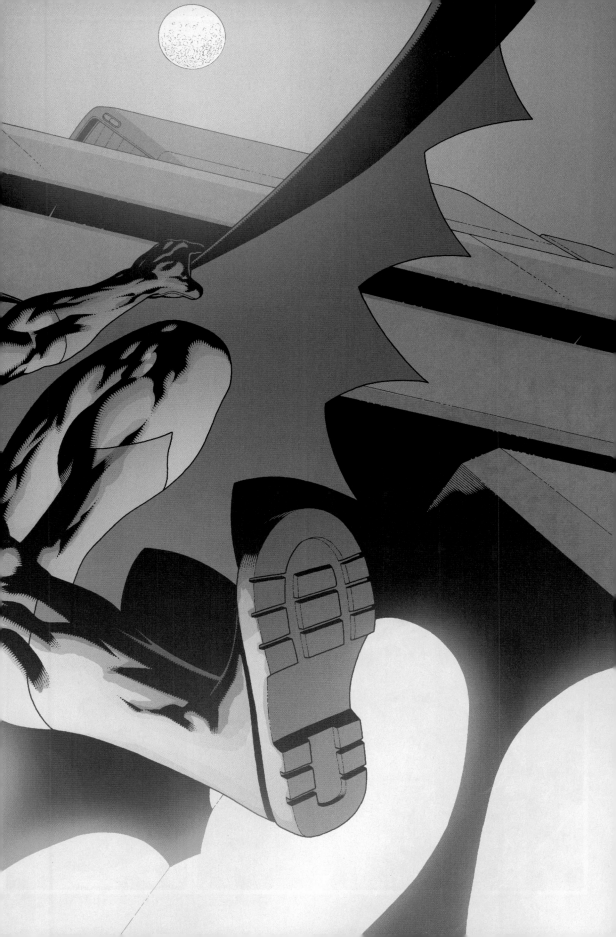

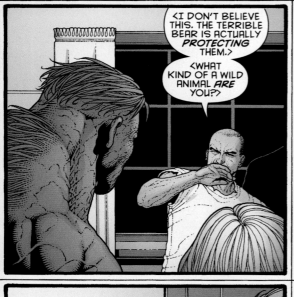

&lt;I DON'T BELIEVE THIS. THE TERRIBLE BEAR IS ACTUALLY *PROTECTING* THEM.&gt;

&lt;WHAT KIND OF A WILD ANIMAL *ARE* YOU?&gt;

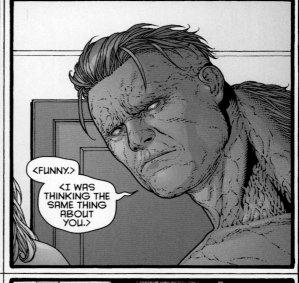

&lt;FUNNY.&gt;

&lt;I WAS THINKING THE SAME THING ABOUT YOU.&gt;

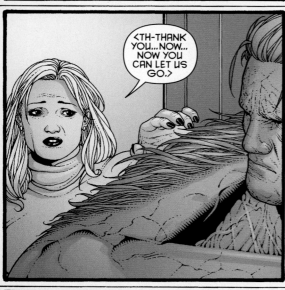

&lt;TH-THANK YOU... NOW... NOW YOU CAN LET US GO.&gt;

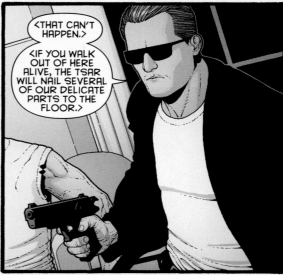

&lt;THAT CAN'T HAPPEN.&gt;

&lt;IF YOU WALK OUT OF HERE ALIVE, THE TSAR WILL NAIL SEVERAL OF OUR DELICATE PARTS TO THE FLOOR.&gt;

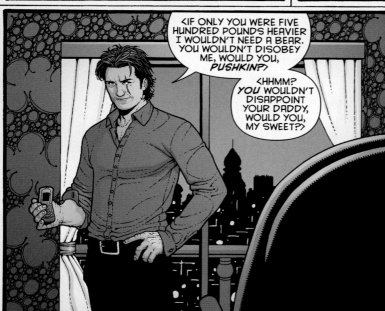

&lt;IF ONLY YOU WERE FIVE HUNDRED POUNDS HEAVIER I WOULDN'T NEED A BEAR. YOU WOULDN'T DISOBEY ME, WOULD YOU, *PUSHKIN?*&gt;

&lt;HHMM? *YOU* WOULDN'T DISAPPOINT YOUR DADDY, WOULD YOU, MY SWEET?&gt;

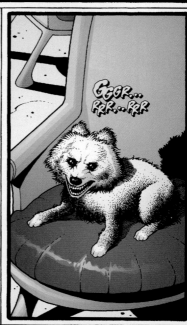

GGGR... RRR... RRR

<GET OUT OF THE WAY. ONE WAY OR ANOTHER, THEY HAVE TO DIE.>
<OH, WE ALL HAVE TO DIE, IGOR. BUT NOT JUST YET.>
BLAM BLAM BLAM
AIEE!
<H-HE'S HIT!>
UGN.
<GUNSHOTS. I'M CALLING IT.>
<LET'S GO!>
<OKAY!>

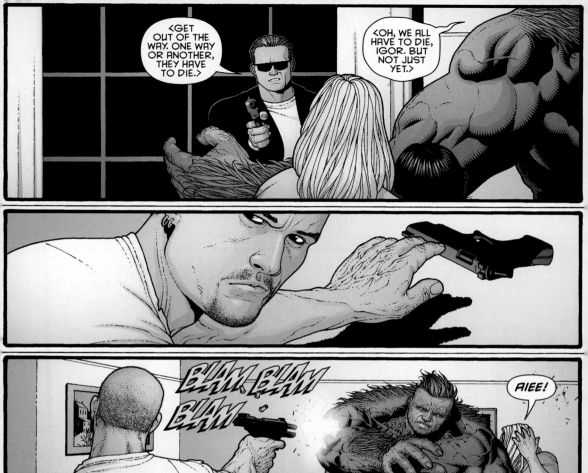

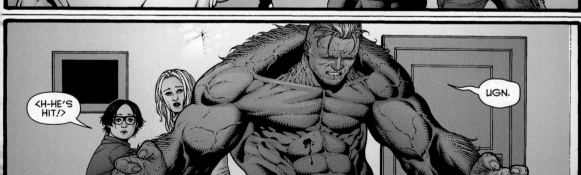

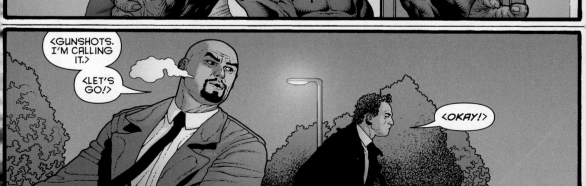

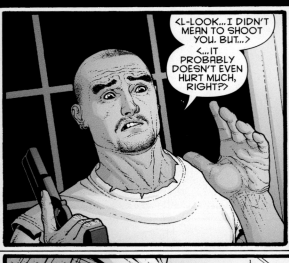

<L-LOOK...I DIDN'T
MEAN TO SHOOT
YOU. BUT...>

<...IT
PROBABLY
DOESN'T EVEN
HURT MUCH,
RIGHT?>

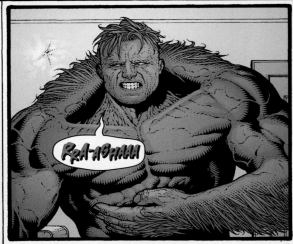

RRA-AGHHHH

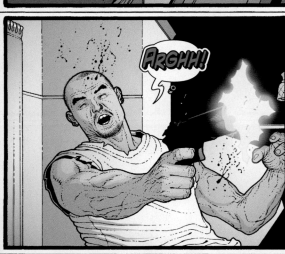

<POLICE!>

<LOOK
AT THAT BIG
FREAK!>

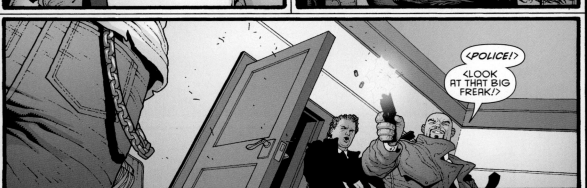

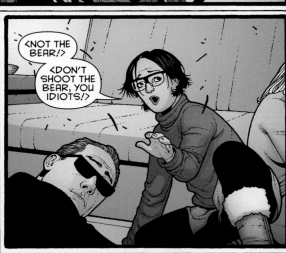

ARGHH!

<NOT THE
BEAR!>

<DON'T
SHOOT THE
BEAR, YOU
IDIOTS!>

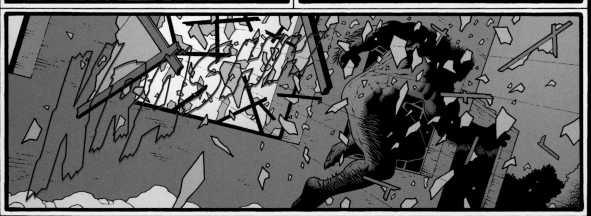

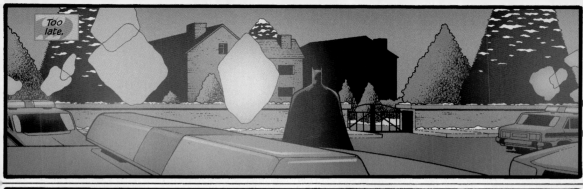

Too late.

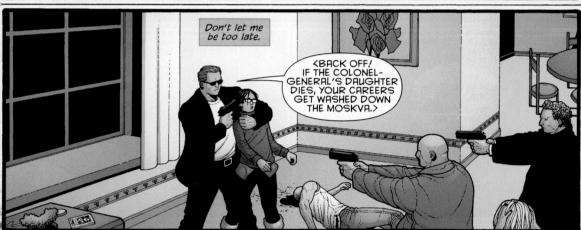

Don't let me be too late.

<BACK OFF! IF THE COLONEL-GENERAL'S DAUGHTER DIES, YOUR CAREERS GET WASHED DOWN THE MOSKVA.>

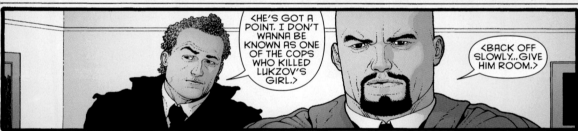

<HE'S GOT A POINT. I DON'T WANNA BE KNOWN AS ONE OF THE COPS WHO KILLED LUKZOV'S GIRL.>

<BACK OFF SLOWLY...GIVE HIM ROOM.>

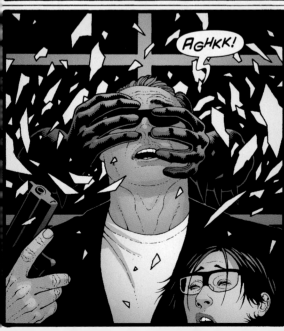

AGHKK!

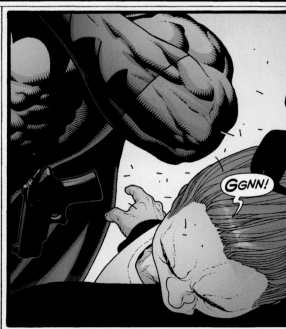

GGNN!

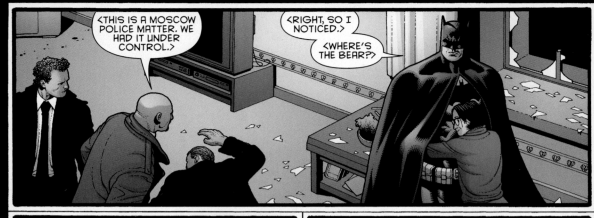

<THIS IS A MOSCOW POLICE MATTER. WE HAD IT UNDER CONTROL.>

<RIGHT, SO I NOTICED.>

<WHERE'S THE BEAR?>

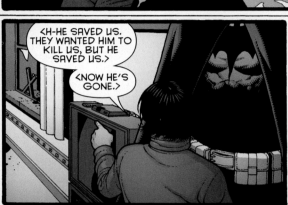

<H-HE SAVED US. THEY WANTED HIM TO KILL US, BUT HE SAVED US.>

<NOW HE'S GONE.>

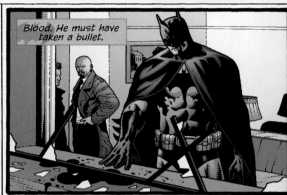

*Blood. He must have taken a bullet.*

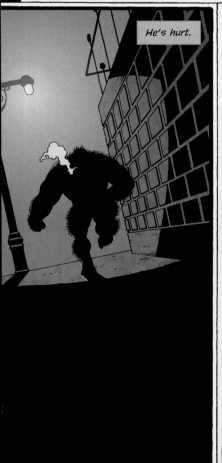

He's hurt.

But how badly?

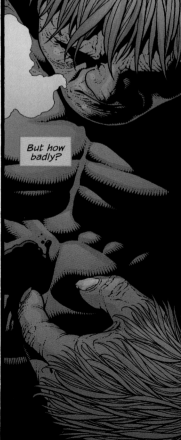

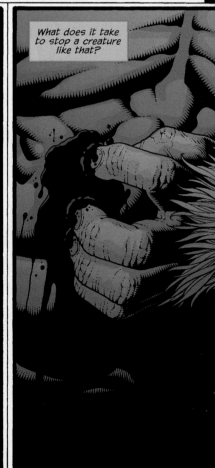

What does it take to stop a creature like that?

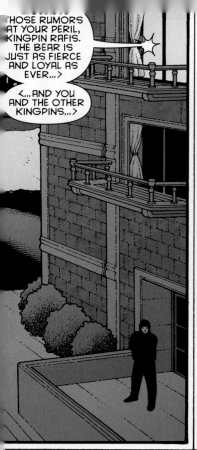

<...THOSE RUMORS AT YOUR PERIL, KINGPIN RAFIS. THE BEAR IS JUST AS FIERCE AND LOYAL AS EVER...>

<...AND YOU AND THE OTHER KINGPINS...>

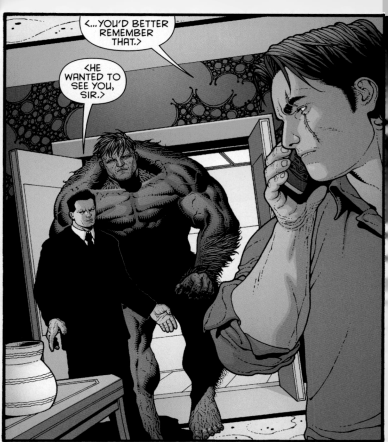

<...YOU'D BETTER REMEMBER THAT.>

<HE WANTED TO SEE YOU, SIR.>

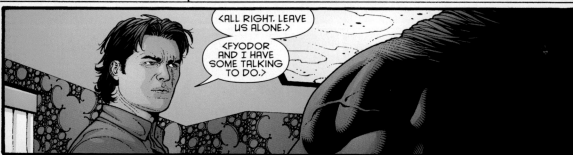

<ALL RIGHT. LEAVE US ALONE.>

<FYODOR AND I HAVE SOME TALKING TO DO.>

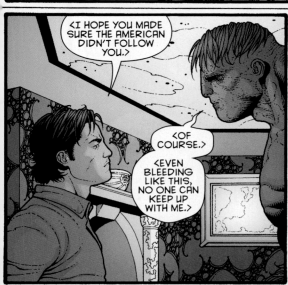

<I HOPE YOU MADE SURE THE AMERICAN DIDN'T FOLLOW YOU.>

<OF COURSE.>

<EVEN BLEEDING LIKE THIS, NO ONE CAN KEEP UP WITH ME.>

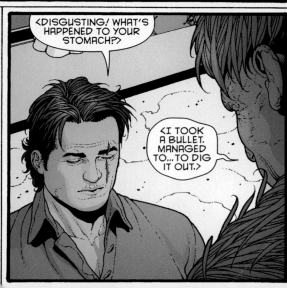

<DISGUSTING! WHAT'S HAPPENED TO YOUR STOMACH?>

<I TOOK A BULLET. MANAGED TO... TO DIG IT OUT.>

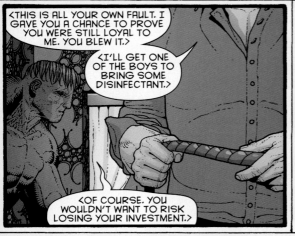

<THIS IS ALL YOUR OWN FAULT. I GAVE YOU A CHANCE TO PROVE YOU WERE STILL LOYAL TO ME. YOU BLEW IT.>

<I'LL GET ONE OF THE BOYS TO BRING SOME DISINFECTANT.>

<OF COURSE. YOU WOULDN'T WANT TO RISK LOSING YOUR INVESTMENT.>

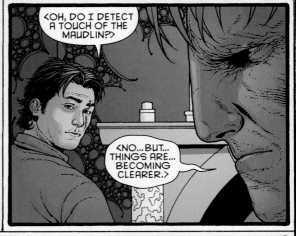

<OH, DO I DETECT A TOUCH OF THE MAUDLIN?>

<NO...BUT... THINGS ARE... BECOMING CLEARER.>

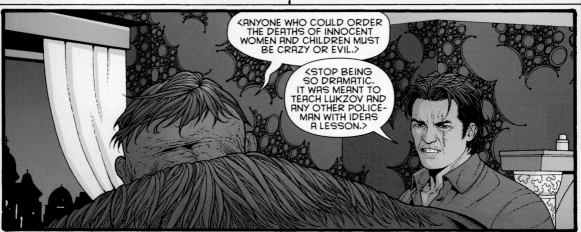

<ANYONE WHO COULD ORDER THE DEATHS OF INNOCENT WOMEN AND CHILDREN MUST BE CRAZY OR EVIL.>

<STOP BEING SO DRAMATIC. IT WAS MEANT TO TEACH LUKZOV AND ANY OTHER POLICE-MAN WITH IDEAS A LESSON.>

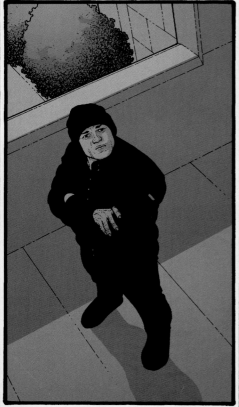

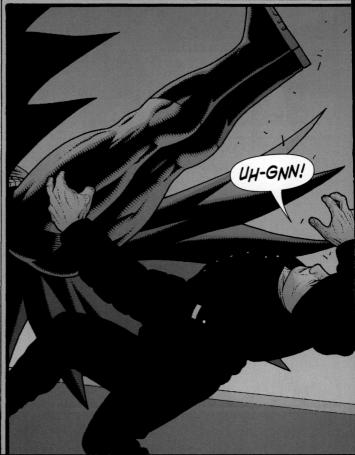

UH-GNN!

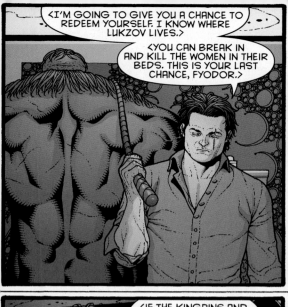

\<I'M GOING TO GIVE YOU A CHANCE TO REDEEM YOURSELF. I KNOW WHERE LUKZOV LIVES.\>

\<YOU CAN BREAK IN AND KILL THE WOMEN IN THEIR BEDS. THIS IS YOUR LAST CHANCE, FYODOR.\>

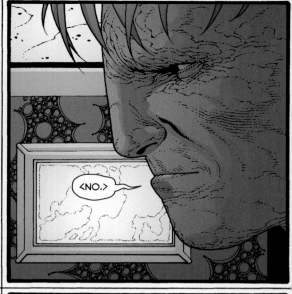

\<NO.\>

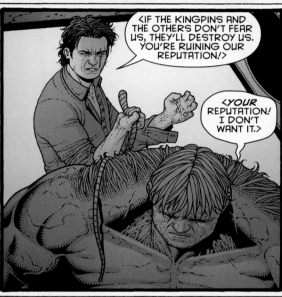

\<IF THE KINGPINS AND THE OTHERS DON'T FEAR US, THEY'LL DESTROY US. YOU'RE RUINING OUR REPUTATION!\>

\<YOUR REPUTATION! I DON'T WANT IT.\>

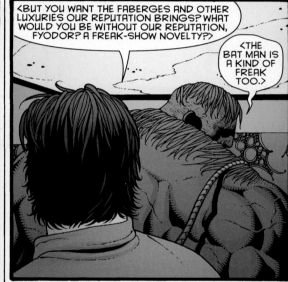

\<BUT YOU WANT THE FABERGES AND OTHER LUXURIES OUR REPUTATION BRINGS? WHAT WOULD YOU BE WITHOUT OUR REPUTATION, FYODOR? A FREAK-SHOW NOVELTY?\>

\<THE BAT MAN IS A KIND OF FREAK TOO.\>

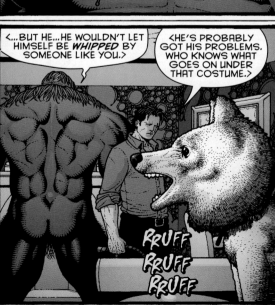

\<...BUT HE...HE WOULDN'T LET HIMSELF BE *WHIPPED* BY SOMEONE LIKE YOU.\>

\<HE'S PROBABLY GOT HIS PROBLEMS. WHO KNOWS WHAT GOES ON UNDER THAT COSTUME.\>

RRUFF RRUFF RRUFF

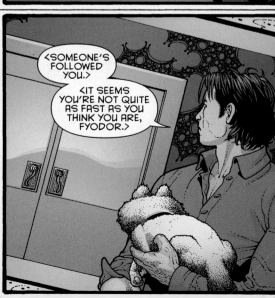

\<SOMEONE'S FOLLOWED YOU.\>

\<IT SEEMS YOU'RE NOT QUITE AS FAST AS YOU THINK YOU ARE, FYODOR.\>

AHHH!
BLAM BLAM
UGN!
<STAVROGIN!>
<IT'S OVER, STAVROGIN.>
<OH, TO BE IN GOTHAM, NOW THAT GOTHAM'S HERE.>

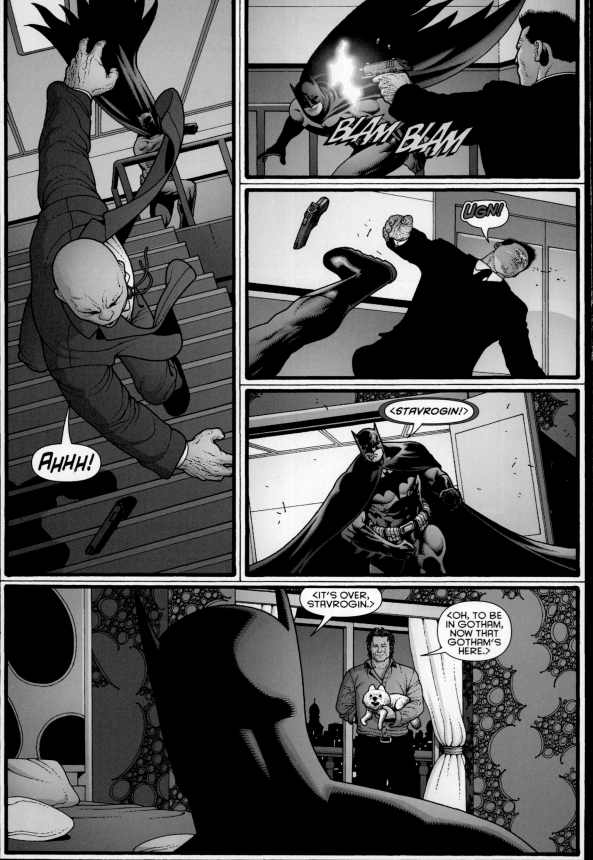

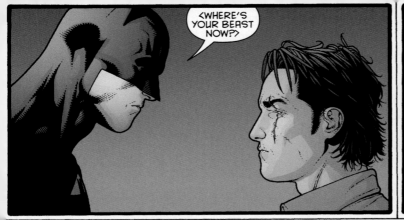

‹WHERE'S YOUR BEAST NOW?›

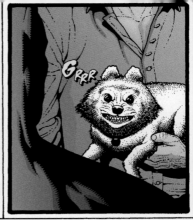

GRRR

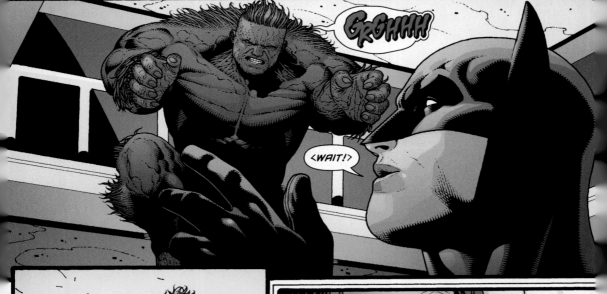

GRGHHH

‹WAIT!›

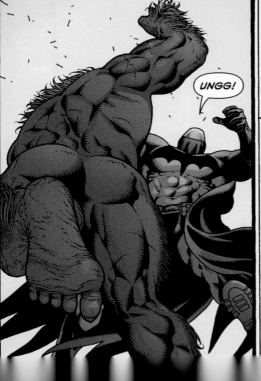

UNGG!

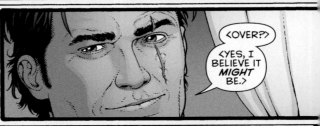

‹OVER?›

‹YES, I BELIEVE IT MIGHT BE.›

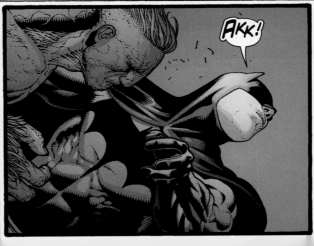

AKK!

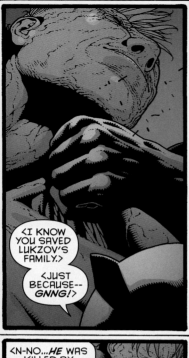

<I KNOW YOU SAVED LUKZOV'S FAMILY.>

<JUST BECAUSE-- GNNG!>

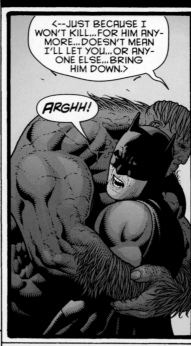

<--JUST BECAUSE I WON'T KILL...FOR HIM ANY-MORE...DOESN'T MEAN I'LL LET YOU...OR ANY-ONE ELSE...BRING HIM DOWN.>

ARGHH!

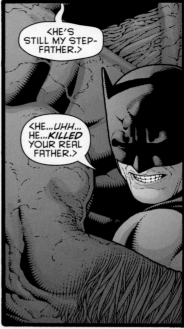

<HE'S STILL MY STEP-FATHER.>

<HE...UHH...HE...KILLED YOUR REAL FATHER.>

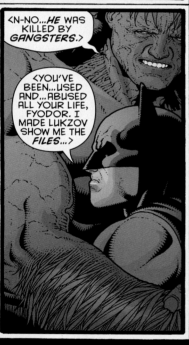

<N-NO...HE WAS KILLED BY GANGSTERS.>

<YOU'VE BEEN...USED AND...ABUSED ALL YOUR LIFE, FYODOR. I MADE LUKZOV SHOW ME THE FILES...>

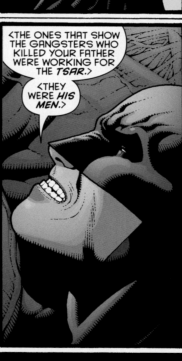

<THE ONES THAT SHOW THE GANGSTERS WHO KILLED YOUR FATHER WERE WORKING FOR THE TSAR.>

<THEY WERE HIS MEN.>

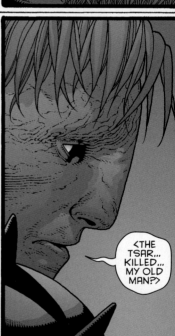

<THE TSAR...KILLED...MY OLD MAN?>

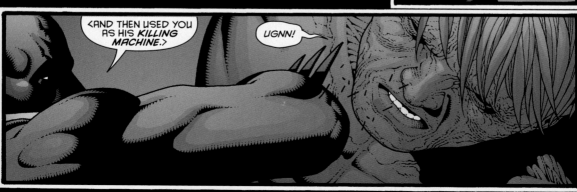

<AND THEN USED YOU AS HIS KILLING MACHINE.>

UGNN!

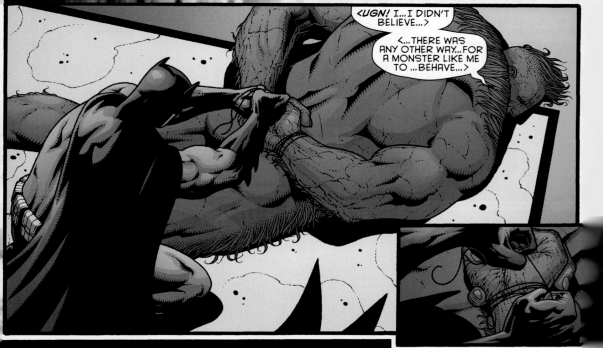

&lt;UGN! I...I DIDN'T BELIEVE...&gt;

&lt;...THERE WAS ANY OTHER WAY...FOR A MONSTER LIKE ME TO ...BEHAVE...&gt;

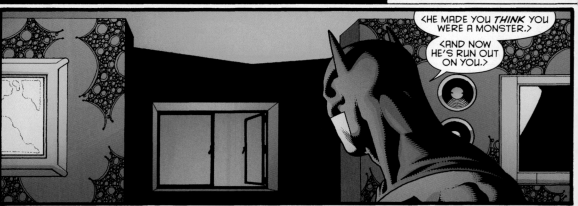

&lt;HE MADE YOU *THINK* YOU WERE A MONSTER.&gt;

&lt;AND NOW HE'S RUN OUT ON YOU.&gt;

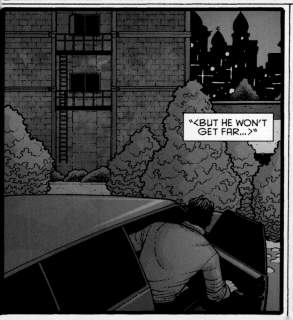

"&lt;BUT HE WON'T GET FAR...&gt;"

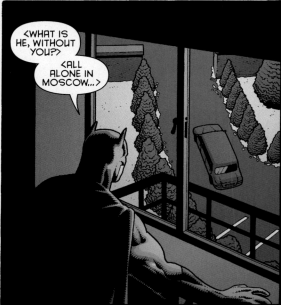

&lt;WHAT IS HE, WITHOUT YOU?&gt;

&lt;ALL ALONE IN MOSCOW...&gt;

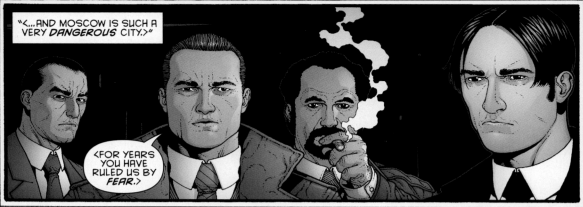

"<...AND MOSCOW IS SUCH A VERY *DANGEROUS* CITY.>"

<FOR YEARS YOU HAVE RULED US BY *FEAR*.>

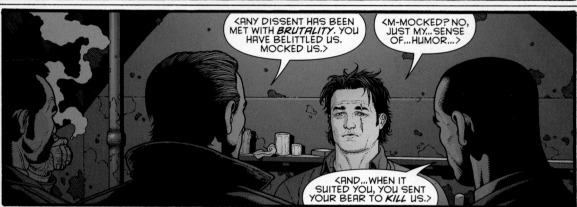

<ANY DISSENT HAS BEEN MET WITH *BRUTALITY*. YOU HAVE BELITTLED US. MOCKED US.>

<M-MOCKED? NO, JUST MY...SENSE OF...HUMOR...>

<AND...WHEN IT SUITED YOU, YOU SENT YOUR BEAR TO *KILL* US.>

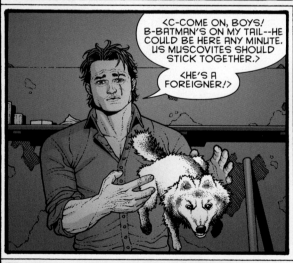

<C-COME ON, BOYS! B-BATMAN'S ON MY TAIL--HE COULD BE HERE ANY MINUTE. US MUSCOVITES SHOULD STICK TOGETHER.>

<HE'S A FOREIGNER!>

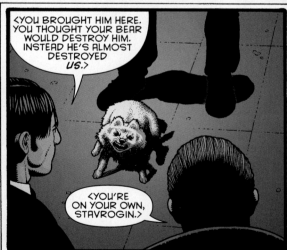

<YOU BROUGHT HIM HERE. YOU THOUGHT YOUR BEAR WOULD DESTROY HIM. INSTEAD HE'S ALMOST DESTROYED *US*.>

<YOU'RE ON YOUR OWN, STAVROGIN.>

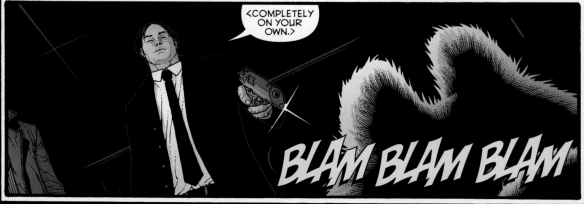

<COMPLETELY ON YOUR OWN.>

BLAM BLAM BLAM

BLAM
<PUSHKY!>
<O-OH... MY...BABY... MY...POOR... POOR...>
<HUH?>
<LOOK WHAT YOU'VE DONE.>
<LOOK WHAT YOU'VE GONE AND DONE!>

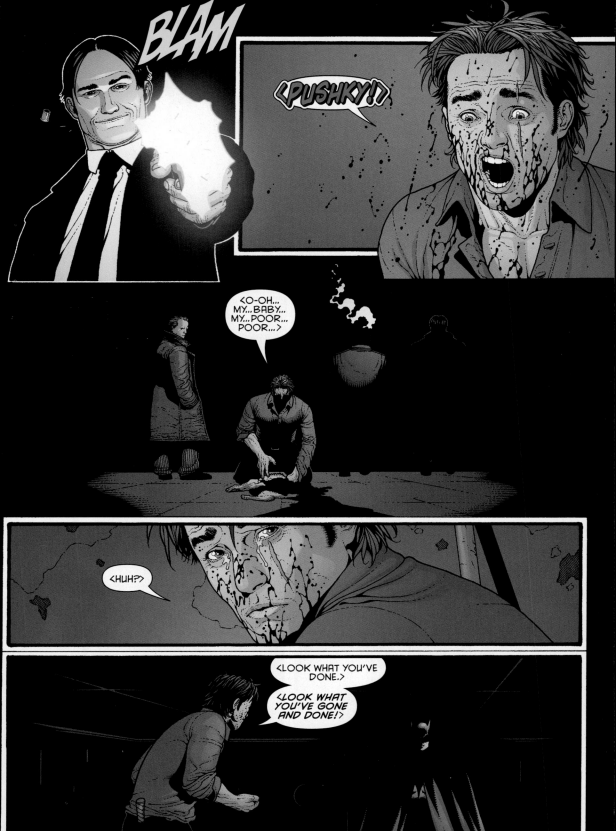

<THIS ISN'T YOUR CITY. THIS IS MY CITY.>
<NOT ANY-MORE.>
<ARROGANT AMERICAN...>
AHH!
<FYODOR! ARE YOU THERE, FYODOR? HELP ME! P-PLEASE HELP! I-I'LL... I'LL BUY YOU MORE FABERGE... I-IF YOU JUST...>
G--GN!
<ALL RIGHT, AMERICAN.>
<YOU WIN.>

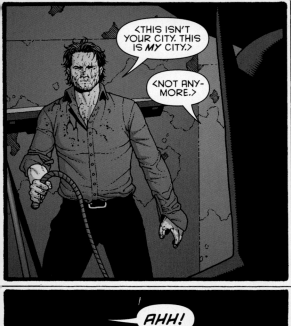

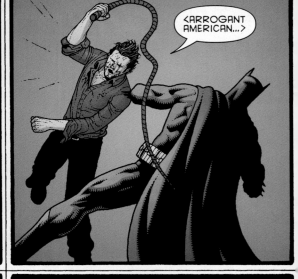

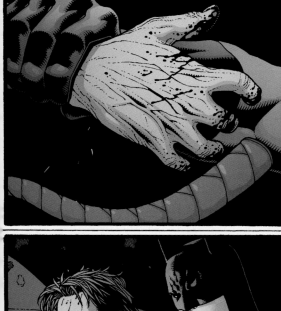

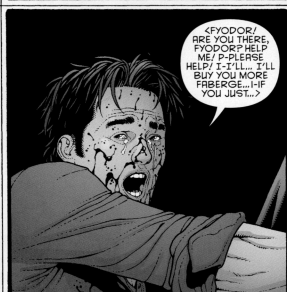

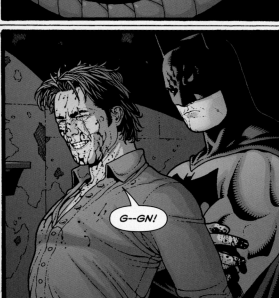

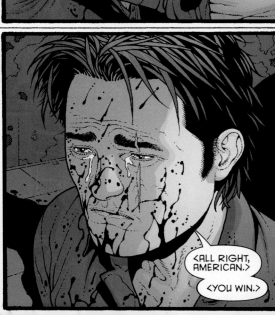

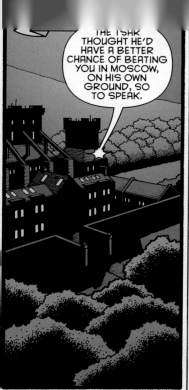

THE TSAR THOUGHT HE'D HAVE A BETTER CHANCE OF BEATING YOU IN MOSCOW, ON HIS OWN GROUND, SO TO SPEAK.

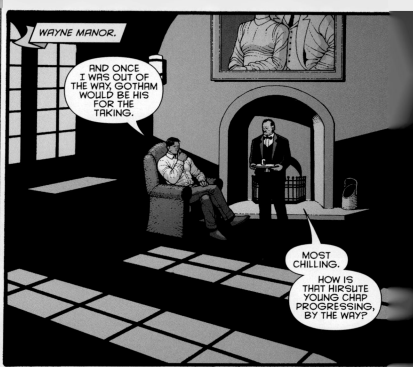

WAYNE MANOR.

AND ONCE I WAS OUT OF THE WAY, GOTHAM WOULD BE HIS FOR THE TAKING.

MOST CHILLING.

HOW IS THAT HIRSUTE YOUNG CHAP PROGRESSING, BY THE WAY?

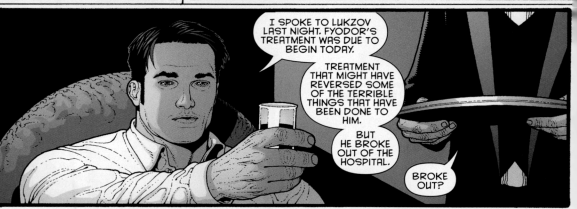

I SPOKE TO LUKZOV LAST NIGHT. FYODOR'S TREATMENT WAS DUE TO BEGIN TODAY.

TREATMENT THAT MIGHT HAVE REVERSED SOME OF THE TERRIBLE THINGS THAT HAVE BEEN DONE TO HIM.

BUT HE BROKE OUT OF THE HOSPITAL.

BROKE OUT?

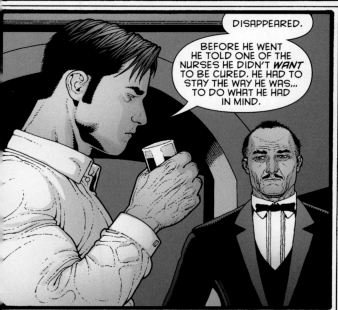

DISAPPEARED.

BEFORE HE WENT HE TOLD ONE OF THE NURSES HE DIDN'T *WANT* TO BE CURED. HE HAD TO STAY THE WAY HE WAS... TO DO WHAT HE HAD IN MIND.

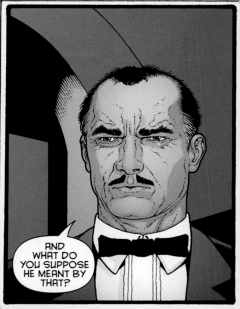

AND WHAT DO YOU SUPPOSE HE MEANT BY THAT?

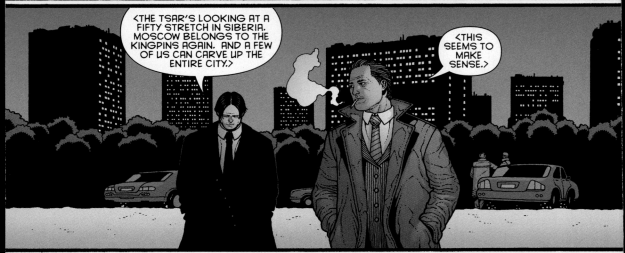

<THE TSAR'S LOOKING AT A FIFTY STRETCH IN SIBERIA. MOSCOW BELONGS TO THE KINGPINS AGAIN. AND A FEW OF US CAN CARVE UP THE ENTIRE CITY.>

<THIS SEEMS TO MAKE SENSE.>

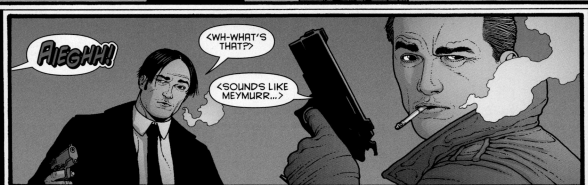

AIEGHH!

<WH-WHAT'S THAT?>

<SOUNDS LIKE MEYMURR...>

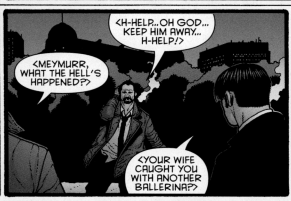

<H-HELP...OH GOD... KEEP HIM AWAY... H-HELP!>

<MEYMURR, WHAT THE HELL'S HAPPENED?>

<YOUR WIFE CAUGHT YOU WITH ANOTHER BALLERINA?>

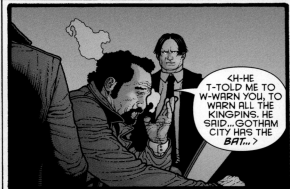

<H-HE T-TOLD ME TO W-WARN YOU, TO WARN ALL THE KINGPINS. HE SAID...GOTHAM CITY HAS THE BAT...>

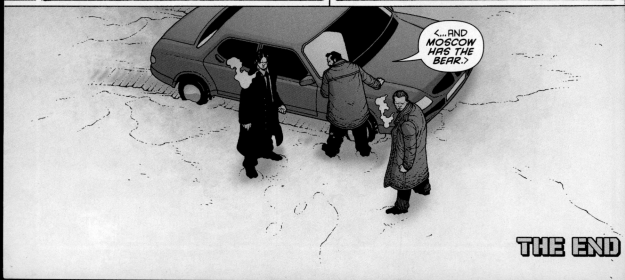

<...AND MOSCOW HAS THE BEAR.>

THE END

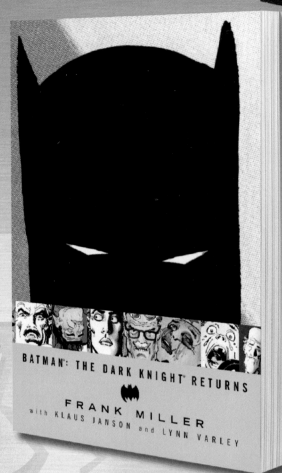
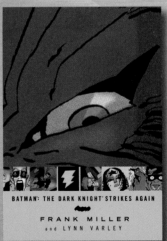
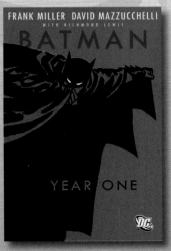
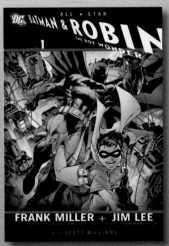

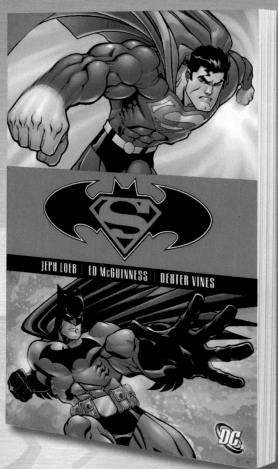
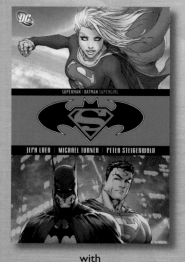
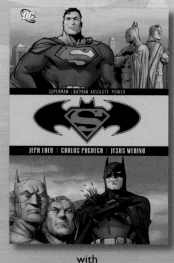
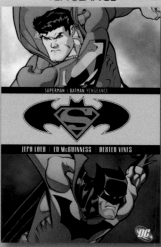

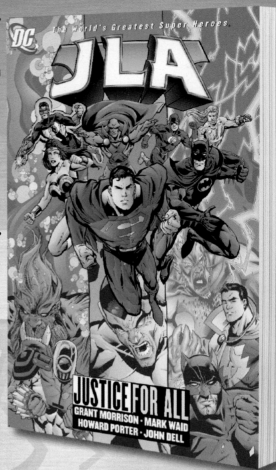
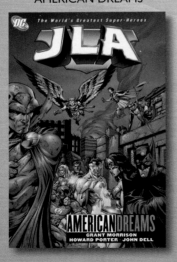
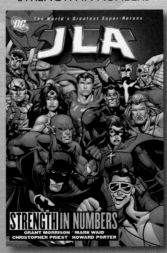
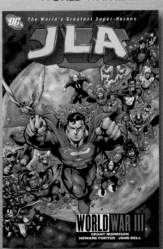